Rhymes and Reasons:

Librarians and Teachers Using Poetry to Foster Literacy

Grades K–6

~ Jane Heitman

Library of Congress Cataloging-in-Publication Data

Heitman, Jane.
    Rhymes and reasons: librarians and teachers using poetry to foster literacy,
grades K–6 / by Jane Heitman.
      p. cm.
    Includes bibliographical references and index.
    ISBN 1-58683-085-6 (Paperback)
    1. Poetry--Study and teaching (Elementary)--Activity programs.   2. English language--Rhyme--Study and teaching (Elementary)--Activity programs.   3. School libraries--Activity programs. 4. Language arts (Elementary)   I. Title.
LB1575.H45 2003
372.64--dc21

                                                                             2003011719

Published by Linworth Publishing, Inc.
480 East Wilson Bridge Road, Suite L
Worthington, Ohio 43085

Copyright © 2003 by Linworth Publishing, Inc.

All rights reserved. Purchasing this book entitles a librarian to reproduce activity sheets for use in the library within a school or entitles a teacher to reproduce activity sheets for a single classroom use within a school. Other portions of the book (up to 15 pages) may be copied for staff development purposes within a single school. Standard citation information should appear on each page. The reproduction of any part of this book for an entire school or school system or for commercial use is strictly prohibited. No part of this book may be electronically reproduced, transmitted, or recorded without written permission from the publisher.

ISBN: 1-58683-085-6
5 4 3 2

Table of Contents

List of Figures viii

Acknowledgements/Dedication ix

Introduction xi

    The Activities xi

    Standards Addressed xii

    Collaboration xii

    How This Book Helps xiii

Chapter 1   A, My Name is Alice: The Alphabet   1

Picture Perfect Poems 1

Acrostics 2

    Acrostic books 3

Anagrams 3

Nonsense poems or foreign language poems 6

Chapter 2   Count on Syllables   9

Haiku 9

Grow a Poe-tree 10

Pond Poems 11

Cinquains 12

    Five Alive 13

Wacky Web Tales 13

Tanka 14

    This Day 14

Rhyme 15

Hear a Rhyme	16
Rhyme Chime	16
Resources	17
Computer Rhymes	17
Resource	18
Rhyme Scheme Detectives	18
Pick a Poem	19
Predict-a-Rhyme	20

Chapter 3   The Wonderful World of Words   21

Word Choice	21
Connotation Conundrum	21
Resources	23
Matching Meanings	24
Where Do Words Come From?	
Etymology & Word Meanings	25
In the Beginning	25
Etymology Forest	28
Resources	29
Alliteration	29
Tongue Twisters	30
Resources	31
Battle of the Tongues	31
Rise and Fall	31
Word Swap	32
Assonance	33
Color Code It	34
Vowel Speak	34
Onomatopoeia	35
Name that Sound	35
Resources	36
Diamante	36
Batter Up!	37
Computer Baseball	39
Reflection Poems	39
Diamond Graphics	41
Go Fly a Diamante!	41
Resources	42

Style 42
    Grammar Matters. 42
    Style Awhile 44
    The Fashion Runway 45

Chapter 4 A Turn of Phrase — 47

Observe, Describe. 47

Concrete Poetry 48
    Concrete ABC 49
    Poetry Room 49
    Really Concrete Poetry 50

Metaphor. 50
    Color Me Poetry 50
    Weather or Not 51
    Moonstruck. 53
    Pop, Pop, Pop 56

Simile 58
    It's Like This 58
    I Am 60
    Like, As, Is 60

Personification. 61
    In Living Color 62
    Personification Improvisation 62
    Picture This. 62
    If I Were a... 63

Repetition 63
    I've Told You a Thousand Times 64
    Echo 66
    Potato Puppets 67
    Raining Refrains 67
    Chorus 68

Rhythm 68
    I Got Rhythm 69
    Jump! 69
    Rap It Up 71

Chapter 5   I Think I Can, I Think I Can: Thoughts   73

Nursery Rhymes..73

Extra, Extra!...75

Teaching Tales..75

Teaching Tales II..76

Word Order, Anyone?.......................................76

Narrative Poems and Choruses............................77
   Musical Stories..77
   Poetic History...79
   Celebrate the Day......................................79
   Chart the Story..80
   It's Story Time..82

Dramatic Monologues......................................83
   Take a Letter..84
   Who's Who?...84
   Who Are These Guys?..................................85

Dramatization...85
   Choral Reading..85
      Resources..86
   Reader's Theater......................................87
      Resources..89
   Full Dramatization....................................89
      Resources..91

Chapter 6   I Feel Pretty: Feelings   93

Happiness...93

Sadness...93

Loneliness..94

Anger..94

Peacefulness..94

Hope..94

Fear...95

Confidence	95
Like/Love	96
Dislike/Hate	96
Mood Quilt	97
Opposing Moods	97
In the Mood	97
Emotion Motion	98
Emotional Temperature	98
Happiness Scale	98
Emote Yourself	99
Happiness	99
Sadness	99
Loneliness	99
Anger	100
Peacefulness	100
Hope	100
Fear	100
Confidence	100
Like/Love	100
Dislike/Hate	100

Glossary 101

Bibliography 103

    Resources to use with Students 103

    Resources for the Library Media Specialist and Teacher 107

    Web sites 108

Author/Title Index 113

Subject Index 119

About the Author 121

List of Figures

Figure 2.1 *Prefixes and Suffixes Table* 12

Figure 3.1 *Connotation Conundrum* 22

Figure 3.2 *In the Beginning* 27

Figure 3.3 *Diamante Template* 38

Figure 3.4 *Diamante* 40

Figure 3.5 *Grammar Matters* 43

Figure 4.1 *Weather or Not* 52

Figure 4.2 *Out in Space* 55

Figure 4.3 *Pop, Pop, Pop* 57

Figure 4.4 *It's Like This* 59

Figure 4.5 *I've Told You* 65

Figure 4.6 *It's Raining Refrains!* 68

Figure 5.1 *Nursery Rhyme Template* 74

Figure 5.2 *The Shape of a Story* 81

Acknowledgements

Thank you to the following who provided expert advice: Linda Armstrong, Maria Ceretti, Lynette Christiansen, Maxine Curley, Vicki Hardy, Judy Harrington, Karen Larsen, Karen McKee, Janet Noland, Connie Parrish, Karen Schniederjan, Pat Schniederjan, Viki Simmons, and Shirley Sternola. Thank you to the following for professional support: Becky Bernal, Jo Hunter, Tom Harris, Chuck Locke, Olivia Buttars, and Brooke Smith. Thank you to the following for encouragement: Bruce Heitman, Eileen Bird, Meg and David Cooper, Ann Gibson, Anne Knipe, Virginia LaCrone, Evelyn Logan, L. Waters, Nancy Wilson, and the WarriorPoets. Special thanks to my editor, Donna Miller.

Dedication

For my parents, Bud and Harriet Anderson, and in memory of my teacher, Bernice Larsen, who made poetry and reading a fun, rewarding part of my life.

Introduction

"If I feel physically as if the top of my head were taken off, I know that is poetry," Emily Dickinson wrote. Poetry packs an emotional wallop by using strong, condensed language written in lines rather than paragraphs. Most poems are relatively short, so students are not overwhelmed with text. Poetry appeals to readers' imaginations and senses. In poetry, rhythm and sound (and sometimes looks) contribute to the meaning. Poetry takes many forms, some of them rhyming. All of these qualities make poetry a good catalyst for helping students understand and appreciate written and oral language. "Poetry really is a great tool for struggling readers because it is predictable, and it flows," Connie Parrish, elementary school teacher, said (Parrish, Connie. "Calling on My Expert Panel." E-mail to Jane Heitman. 15 Apr. 2002).

The Activities

This book gives library media specialists and teachers poetry-based, inexpensive activities that provide practice and reinforcement of language elements. Unless otherwise noted, activities are adaptable to grades kindergarten through six to be conducted in the library, classroom, or both.

Some activities are designed especially for pre- and beginning readers. Other activities can be adapted for this age group using these techniques:

- Have students work orally,
- Have students respond with gestures or movements rather than writing,
- Write students' responses for them,
- Use visual aids when possible (For more information about adapting activities to various age groups, see Collom 193.)

Library media specialists, teachers, or both lead activities. Activities appeal to a variety of skill levels, interest areas, and learning styles. They can be done in any order. Some activities take part of a class period; some take longer. Some require a lot of adult direction; some require students' independent research. Some assign students to write poems individually; some assign the teacher to lead a class collaborative poem. (For tips on leading class collaborative poetry writing, see Collom 232.) Most of the activities take little poetry knowledge or preparation. Unless otherwise noted, the only supplies needed are paper and pencils. Poster board or newsprint paper and markers or crayons may be desired to create larger works.

As much as possible, the library media specialist or teacher should assign preparation tasks to students, making the project truly theirs.

Many activities lend themselves to display. Here are some display suggestions:
- Bulletin board
- School Web page
- Hall or wall mural

Poems for each activity are suggested, with one source given and more listed in the bibliography. Poems selected for activities are found in many anthologies or online, making them readily available. They were selected for their quality, appropriateness, and ability to demonstrate a particular language arts concept. Book and Web site recommendations were made by first-hand experience and referrals from library media specialists, teachers, and other education experts. All Web sites were checked immediately prior to publication, but readers will need to re-check them before using them in activities. Books listed in the bibliography are in print at the time of this writing, unless they are marked "OP" (out of print).

Standards Addressed

Each activity lists American Association of School Librarians (AASL) Information Literacy Standards and National Council of Teachers of English (NCTE) standards applications. The standards and more information about them are found at AASL <www.ala.org/aasl/ip_nine.html> and NCTE <www.ncte.org/standards/standards.shtml>.

A bibliography of print and Web resources and two indexes, author/title and subject increase usability.

Collaboration

Making connections across the curriculum is encouraged. Many activities direct the library media specialist to work with a teacher in conducting the lesson. "The mission of the library media program is to ensure that students and staff are effective users of ideas and information. This mission is accomplished… by working with other educators to design learning strategies to meet the needs of individual students" (*Information* 6). Today's library media specialists, teachers, administrators, and students partner with each other in the learning process to achieve educational goals.

How this happens in reality varies. The role any of the partners takes depends upon the school's leadership and desires, the rapport among the partners, and individual styles and personalities. In general, library media specialists are the resources experts; teachers are the curricular experts. Many partners have devised lesson-planning templates, detailing standards covered and duties and expectations of each partner. Finding common planning time and developing appropriate library scheduling can be great challenges. Work with your administrative partner to find solutions. Together, all the partners can create and refine enjoyable lessons that support standards and fulfill curriculum requirements. For more on collaboration, see Buzzeo, Glandon, and *Information Power*.

How This Book Helps

This book has already done most of the planning for you. Activity extensions and variations allow for a variety of leadership styles. You have only to decide which activities fit your needs and styles, and who leads what, when, and where. A teacher may do the initial teaching of the concept, and the library media specialist will reinforce it with the activity. The teacher and library media specialist may simultaneously lead group activities in the library. The library media specialist may plan and deliver the entire lesson and activity, or the teacher may.

Decide these logistics, and gather poems and a few materials. You are ready to improve your students' literacy skills for life.

Chapter 1   A, My Name is Alice: The Alphabet

As the first building block of written language, the alphabet is essential. The way the letters look, the sounds they make, and the way they interact to become words are all part of the decoding process. Library media specialists and teachers can reinforce alphabet knowledge with several simple poetry-related activities.

Picture Perfect Poems

For grades K–2

 Materials needed: old magazines, catalogs, and calendars; tape; newsprint or large paper

Supports AASL Information Literacy Standards 1, 2, 3, 6, 9
American Association of School Librarians Literacy Standards
<www.ala.org/aasl/ip_nine.html>
Supports NCTE Standards 3, 6, 8, 11, 12
National Council of Teachers of English Standards
<www.ncte.org/standards/standards.shtml>

This activity will reinforce alphabet recognition and the ability to connect the letter with the object it represents.

Choose a letter of the alphabet. Have students find and cut out pictures of items that begin with that letter. When all students have found at least one picture, have them show their picture and say what it is. The library media specialist or teacher can write the word on the board, underlining the first letter for emphasis. Then the leader can guide them in "writing" a poem using the pictures. Choose a student to tape his or her picture to the large paper. This will begin your poem. Ask the students what they can say about that subject with the pictures they have chosen. Have students add their pictures as appropriate. The library media specialist or teacher can write in necessary words between the pictures. Have the class recite their poem together.

Variations

Following the directions above,

- Have students write individual or small group poems. The library media specialist or teacher will circulate among the students to help with accuracy and words not pictured.

- Use a flannel board or computer program to write picture poems.

- Use real objects available in the room rather than cutting out pictures. Set them in their chosen poetic order, placing words in between on tag board folded so that it will stand up.

- Prepare pictures of familiar objects beginning with a variety of letters. Students can choose from them rather than cutting out their own.

～Acrostics

An acrostic begins with a word spelled out. Then each letter of the word is used to begin another word or phrase, creating a poem.

Acrostic poems creatively reinforce letter recognition, spelling, and vocabulary. In addition, the acrostic activities below help students evaluate texts and apply conventional language skills.

Supports AASL Information Literacy Standards 1, 3, 5, 9

Supports NCTE Standards 3, 5, 6, 11, 12

Acrostic poems can be created as a group or by individual students. Have students write their names, one letter on each line of notebook paper, one letter beneath the other. (Depending on the students' ability levels, library media specialists or teachers may reinforce the name, shape, and sound of letters with students.) Then have them write a word or phrase beside each letter that begins with that letter and describes them. Library media specialists or teachers can show how to use the dictionary to find appropriate words.

An example:

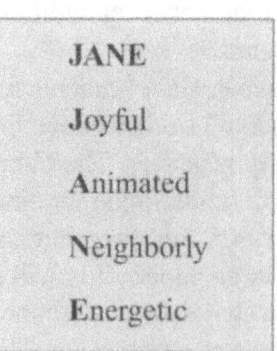

Allow students to decorate and display in the library or classroom, or on their lockers or desks.

Variations

- Ask students to "act out" their acrostic, using their bodies to make the shape of the initial letter, then acting out the word they have chosen, then shaping the next initial letter, and so on. Students enjoy making name acrostics to take home for each family member and friends.
- Collaborate with the art teacher to create decorative acrostics.
- Collaborate with the computer technician to create computer-graphically enhanced acrostics.

- Use acrostics in content areas by choosing a word related to a specific subject, such as a science term or historical figure.

- Use seasonal words (spring, summer, fall, winter), holiday words (Valentine, etc.), days of the week, months of the year. These topics are especially suitable for group collaboration, decoration, and display.

- Choose a somewhat long, but common word (perhaps from that week's vocabulary or spelling list). Assign each student a letter. He or she chooses a word to go along with the letter. When everyone is finished, see what acrostic poems the group can create using their letters and words. Have them stand in correct letter order to spell the word they have come up with (It may not be the same as your original word!) and recite their letter and word. If you like, you can expand this activity by asking about the meaning of the poem they have created. Would other descriptors fit the topic better? Can another word be created from the letters?

- Find "acrostic" music, such as "MOTHER" ("'M' is for the many ...") or "LOVE" ("'L' is for the way you Look at me ..."). Play it or sing it with your students. Then have them put their acrostic poems to the same tune, a different tune, or a tune they make up.

Resources

 Books:

Hummon, David. *Animal Acrostics,* Nevada City, CA: Dawn, 1999.

Schnur, Steven. *Autumn: an Alphabet Acrostic,* NY: Clarion, 1997.

—. *Spring: an Alphabet Acrostic,* NY: Clarion, 1999.

—. *Summer: an Alphabet Acrostic,* NY: Boston, MA: Houghton, 2001.

—. *Winter: an Alphabet Acrostic,* NY: Clarion, 2002.

ᴀ*Anagrams*

An anagram uses letters from one word to create a different word. Working with anagrams helps students recognize that letters make up words and individual letters may sound different in different words.

The anagram activities below include creative student group work and application of textual features and language principles. Library media specialists leading these activities are helping students access information accurately and creatively.

Supports AASL Information Literacy Standards 1, 3, 5, 9

Supports NCTE Standards 3, 6, 11,12

Anagram poems can be created by individual students or as a group. Begin by choosing a word, perhaps one from the current spelling or vocabulary list. For individual students: Have students write the word at the top of their papers. Ask them to make as many words as they can from the letters in the top word. They should write these in a list below the word on top. For example: How many words can you find in this word?

Conversation

Here are some of the possibilities:

art	ratio	sate	raver
cart	rat	onto	raves
car	tin	on	stave
soon	nation	to	vase
coon	near	sat	
noon	train	ion	
ration	voice	rave	

Now, have students use the original word as the title of a poem. Have them choose words from their word list to write a short poem about the topic. Here is an example from the list above:

Conversation

I sat in the train station near noon,

listening to a tin voice

rave on about the

ratio of rations

in the nation.

Soon, I got onto my car.

    Have students underline the words from their lists. Ask them to read their words, and then their poems aloud. While they read, ask the other students to listen for certain letters. In the case of this example, ask them to listen for the "t." Though the students will not have the poem in front of them, they should be able to recognize at least some. Talk about the different sounds the "t" took in this poem.
    To do this activity with a group, put the original word on the board and have students either call out anagrams or come forward and write them on the board.

When you are finished with your list, create a class poem, and write it on the board. Discuss how certain letters sound, as above.

Do the activity above on the computer by putting the original word in a word processing program, and having students type in their anagrams. Create a class poem, as above, and type it in the computer. If possible, project the image as the activity takes place.

Variations

- To turn this activity into a game, choose a word and have the students write it at the top of their papers. Have them create their anagrams lists. When everyone is ready, have the class stand. Have a student slowly read his or her list. Anyone else who had that word on his or her list should sit. Move on to the next student and continue until each student has a turn. If students are already seated when it is their turn, they should stand and read words from their lists that have not been heard yet. Based on the word list from those left standing at the end, create a class poem, giving those seated first chance at saying or writing lines.

- Play anagrams using Scrabble® games. Either set up a Scrabble® set for every four students, or set up one or two stations where students can play. When they have completed the game, students can create poems from the words. These poems should be recited or posted in front of the entire class.

- A variation on the above activity is to draw a large Scrabble® board on newsprint paper. Make squares and write letters on them, using the Scrabble® letter distribution and including blanks for wild cards. (Students can help with this.) Post the Scrabble® board on a classroom or library wall or bulletin board. Put the Scrabble® "tiles" in a box or basket next to the board. Have tape or a glue stick available. Put an interesting word in the center, and let students take turns adding words by drawing five "tiles" out of the box. Unused "tiles" go back in the box. When everyone has had a turn, create a class poem, using the original word as the title, and added words as poem elements.

- A variation on the above is to leave the giant Scrabble® board up and invite students to add a letter or word when they have spare moments of inspiration. Allow students to place letters over other letters. Let it grow, and see what happens! You (or your designee) may like to keep a list of words used, so that when most of the letters are on the board, you can create a poem with them.

- Scrabble® is available as computer software, produced by Infogrames <http://us.infogrames.com>. If you have it, you can adapt the activities above for students to create at the computer.

~Nonsense or Foreign Language Poems

Using nonsense poems such as Lewis Carroll's "Jabberwocky" or poems in foreign languages helps reinforce phonics techniques and contextual reading. This is a springboard from the anagram work above where you have shown how the same letter can sound different depending on which letters are its neighbors.

Supports AASL Information Literacy Standards 1, 2, 3, 5,9

Supports NCTE Standards 3, 6, 9, 11, 12

Give students copies of a nonsense poem, such as Lewis Carroll's "Jabberwocky." The following activities use "Jabberwocky" as a basis, but you can use other appropriate poems for the same, or very similar, activities.

Ask students to read it silently and circle words they do not know. Explain that the author made up words, so nobody knows what all the words mean. When they are finished, ask them to work in pairs, and read the poem to each other. When they are finished, ask what words they found difficult. How would they pronounce them? Review phonics strategies, going over each difficult word, with everyone saying the word aloud.

This is a good opportunity to point out that new words come into our language each year. People make them up! "Chortle" is word Carroll made up for "Jabberwocky." Now it is in the dictionary. Ask the class how they would pronounce "chortle"? What does the dictionary say? Library media specialists can teach students how to read dictionary pronunciation keys.

Ask students if they or anyone they know has made up a word. What was the word and what was the meaning? How would it be spelled? (Recommend *Frindle* by Andrew Clement to interested students or read it to students.)

You may discuss meanings for made-up words, considering context. For instance, what does a jub-jub bird look like? Have students draw it or other characters or scenes from the poem. They may like to make their art work three-dimensional by adding yarn, foil, feathers, glitter, buttons, etc. (Bring these supplies in yourself, or collaborate with your art teacher.) The library media specialist can assist students in using computers to create their images. Have students show their work and explain why they made the scene look the way they did.

You might like to have a guest reader (another faculty member or parent) read the poem to the class after the class has worked on it. Ask the class to listen for difficult words. Did the reader pronounce them the same way you did? This gives an opportunity to mention that some words have more than one correct pronunciation. The library media specialist can show students variant pronunciations for such words as "either," "tomato," and "coyote." In the case of made-up words, nobody but the author knows, so there is no wrong answer!

Choose a foreign language poem (preferably one in a language that is not native to anyone in the class) that you can also find on tape or have someone fluent in the language read on tape. Give students written copies and have them "read" it silently, circling words they do not know. Then have them work with a partner and read it out loud to each other. Now play the tape and have students follow along. How did your pronunciations compare to the tape? Explain that you have applied English phonics strategies to another language, and that often does not work. You may like to discuss the sounds you heard, hard and soft, vowels and consonants, etc. Which sounds did you like? Which sounds did you not like?

Resources

 Books:

Nonsense poems can be found in:

Cole, William, comp. *Oh, What Nonsense!* NY: Puffin, 1990.

Ferris, Helen, comp. *Favorite Poems Old and New,* Garden City, NY: Doubleday, 1957.

Hale, Glorya. *Read-Aloud Poems for Young People,* NY: Black Dog & Leventhal, 1997.

Prelutsky, Jack, comp. *The Random House Book of Poetry*, NY: Random, 1983.

Individual nonsense poems that work well with the activities above are:

Carroll, Lewis. "Jabberwocky." (Hale 175)

Lear, Edward. "The Pobble Who Has No Toes." (Hale 192)

Milligan, Spike. "On the Ning Nang Nong." (Prelutsky *Random* 171)

Richards, Laura E. "Eletelephony." (Prelutsky *Random* 192)

Turner, Nancy Byrd. "Contrary Mary." (Hale 376)

Chapter 2   Count on Syllables

Syllables, the second building block in creating words, help students break unknown words into parts. Prefixes and suffixes provide meaning clues. Syllable placement within a word gives pronunciation clues. These activities, focusing on syllables, empower students to tackle decoding longer words.

In the activities below, students apply their language skills to a variety of poetic forms by both reading and writing them. The library media specialist and teacher help students use information accurately and creatively.

Haiku

Supports AASL Information Literacy Standards 2, 3, 5, 9

Supports NCTE Standards 1, 3, 4, 5, 6, 9, 11, 12

Haiku are three-line traditional Japanese poems, usually about nature. They do not often rhyme. They may have a surprise at the end. The first line is five syllables long, the second line is seven syllables, the third is five syllables. Working with haiku helps students understand what a syllable is. Reading, writing, and hearing haiku helps students see how syllables work together to create a beautiful image. Note that in English, the five-seven-five syllable format is not always followed. Translations from Japanese sometimes need more or fewer syllables per line to keep the author's meaning.

Introduce haiku to your students by defining the form and giving them examples. Also define "syllable." Together, count the number of syllables per line. You might have students clap or tap syllables out as they are being read. Then consider the topic and meaning or image. Ask questions such as, "What does this say about nature? Does it say anything about the world in general?" Read many samples aloud, giving students turns at reading. Count the syllables of each line. This activity can be team-taught, with the classroom teacher beginning the lesson and the library media specialist reading haiku and providing resources.

Here is an example from the classic haiku poet Issa:

> A red morning sky,
> For you, snail;
> Are you glad about it?
> (Lewis 2.)

Resources

Books:

Other books containing haiku:

Gollub, Matthew. *Cool Melons—Turn to Frogs! The Life and Poems of Issa,* NY: Lee, 1998.

Janeczko, Paul B., sel. *Stone Bench in an Empty Park,* NY: Grolier, 2000.

Koch, Kenneth and Kate Farrell. *Talking to the Sun: An Illustrated Anthology of Poems for Young People,* NY: Metropolitan Museum of Art and Holt, 1985.

Web Sites:

Ramsey, Inez. *Forms of Poetry for Children.* James Madison U. 5 Dec. 2002 <http://falcon.jmu.edu/~ramseyil/poeform.htm>. (Click on Haiku.)

Suzuki, Ryo, Ed. Children's Haiku Garden. 9 Nov. 2002. 5 Dec. 2002 <www.tecnet.or.jp/~haiku/>. (Click on Ryo's Message for details)

Poetry Collections, Poetic Forms & Styles, and Poets. 1 Dec. 2002. Web English Teacher. 5 Dec. 2002. <www.webenglishteacher.com/poetry.html>. (Click on Poetry Forms for lesson plans and activities.)

Write a class haiku or two for practice. Then have students write their own. Encourage them to adhere to the five-seven-five format. When they have written two or three, have students work with a partner. They should read each other's haiku and count the syllables in each line. Also have them consider the topic and image. Have them make suggestions for improvement, if necessary, and allow time for revising.

Grow a Poe-tree

 ***Materials needed:*** big brown paper, green paper, markers, tape

Supports AASL Standards 2, 3, 4, 5, 6

Supports NCTE Standards 3, 4, 6, 11, 12

Take advantage of haiku's natural tradition by having students create a Poe-tree. The library media specialist, students, and art teacher make a wall-sized tree trunk from brown paper. Affix the tree to a wall, leaving room for many leaves at the ends of the branches. Cut out large colored leaves, at least one per student. Have students choose their best haiku and write it on their leaf in black marker.

Then they can attach the leaf to the tree, for all to read and enjoy. The Poe-tree is an excellent tool for displaying students' work on parents' night or for open houses, and it can help attract these visitors to the library.

Variations

- Design the tree trunk and leaves to reflect a type of tree in your geographic area.
- In spring, make green leaves; in fall, they may be brown, gold, colored. In fall, some leaves can go on the tree and some on the ground.
- If your area gets winter snow, use snowflakes instead of leaves.

∽Pond Poems

Materials needed: child's plastic pool or wall art to look like a pond; card stock, markers; list of words, prefixes, and suffixes; dictionary

Supports AASL Standards 1, 2, 3, 5, 6, 9

Supports NCTE Standards 3, 5, 6, 11, 12

Supply a child's plastic pool or draw a pond on blue paper and attach it to a wall. From card stock, make cards with each containing one prefix or suffix on one side. On the other side, write "Prefix" or "Suffix." Put the card in the pool or attach to the paper pond with "Prefix" or "Suffix" side up. Make "fishing rods" out of card stock, at least one for each student. Write a spelling, vocabulary, or grade-appropriate word on the fishing rod. (Laminate the rods before writing the words, if possible, and write the words with erasable marker, so you can use the rods again with different words.) Before beginning the activity, the library media specialist will review prefixes, suffixes, and their meanings. Show students dictionary entries containing common prefixes and suffixes.

Have each student go to the pond and "fish" for a prefix or suffix and add it to his or her word so that it makes a real word. If the prefix or suffix does not make a real word, the student must "toss it back" into the pond. Have a dictionary ready for challenges.

When all students have gone fishing, put them in groups of four or five. Have them share their "catch of the day." Have each group write a poem together, using their original words or their newly created words. Have groups recite their poems to the class.

Use prefixes and suffixes found in your language arts book, or choose from those listed below.

Prefixes			Suffixes		
Prefix	Meaning	Example	Suffix	Meaning	Example
dis–	apart	disappear	–able	apt to	dosable
ex–	out	export	–ful	full of	healthful
in–	not	incorrect	–hood	state of being	sisterhood
pre–	before	preview	–less	without	penniless
re–	do again	rerun	–ly	in what way	quickly
sub–	below	submarine	–ment	result of action	excitement

Figure 2.1: Prefixes and Suffixes Table

Variation

Have students keep their matches that are not real words and, in groups of four or five, have them make poems of the nonsense words. Ask classmates to guess the meanings based on context.

~Cinquains

Another syllable-counting poem is the cinquain (pronounced sin-KANE), originated by Adelaide Crapsey in the early 1900's. Today's cinquain has developed into a five-line poem with the following pattern:

> two-syllable word giving the title
>
> four syllables describing the title
>
> six syllables expressing an action related to the title
>
> eight syllables expressing a feeling related to the title
>
> two or three syllables giving a different word for the title.
>
> Here is an example:
>
> Star light
>
> Twinkling, glowing
>
> Shooting through the heavens
>
> Makes me feel tiny and awe-struck
>
> Night light.

Five Alive

 Materials needed: Large newsprint paper, markers

Supports AASL Information Literacy Standards 1, 2, 3, 4, 5, 6, 7, 9

Supports NCTE Standards 3, 6, 11, 12

Post newsprint paper across one wall and provide markers for students. Review cinquain structure. Put students in groups of five and have each group line up single file in front of the newsprint. The first student from each group writes line one on the newsprint and passes the marker on to the second student, who writes line two, and so on. Group conferences are okay. When everyone is done, have the groups recite their poems to the class. Students should listen and watch for the correct format.

Variation

 Materials needed: Computer with word processing program, printer

Supports AASL Information Literacy Standards 1, 2, 3, 4, 5, 6, 7, 9

Supports NCTE Standards 3, 6, 8, 11, 12

Do the same activity, only on a computer word processing program, with students keying in their lines. Save the files for future reference. Print the results and recite. Students should listen for the correct format.

Wacky Web Tales

 Materials needed: Computer with Internet access, printer

Supports AASL Information Literacy Standards 1, 2, 3, 4, 5, 6, 7, 9

Supports NCTE Standards 3, 4, 6, 8, 11, 12

Assist students in creating tales using the form at *Wacky Web Tales, Kids' Place*. 1996–2002. Houghton Mifflin Co. 5 Dec. 2002 <www.eduplace.com/tales/index.html>. Read the finished products to the rest of the class or within a smaller group. Ask, "Would you change anything to make the tale better?" "Can you improve on the computer's work?" Allow for revising and post the finished products.

Resource

 *Web Site:*

Ramsey, Inez. Forms of Poetry for Children. James Madison U. 5 Dec. 2002 <http://falcon.jmu.edu/~ramseyil/poeform.htm>. (Click on Cinquains.)

~Tanka

Tanka are 31-syllable Japanese poems written to mark an occasion. In English, the lines are divided like this: five syllables, seven, five, seven, seven. As with haiku, the syllable count is not absolute.

Here is an example by an anonymous Japanese poet:

> When the frost lies white
>
> Upon fields where travelers
>
> Must find their shelter,
>
> O flock of heavenly cranes,
>
> Cover my child with your wings!
>
> (Baron 50)

Since this is a more difficult and complex form, guided practice and class collaboration led by the library media specialist or teacher is recommended. The library media specialist can provide and read examples of tanka.

This Day

 ***Materials needed:*** Library reference materials and Web sites related to special days; board, overhead, or large newsprint; writing tool; computer with Internet access; printer

Supports AASL Information Literacy Standards 1, 2, 3, 4, 5, 6, 7, 9

Supports NCTE Standards 1, 3, 4, 5, 6, 8, 11, 12

Choose an occasion to celebrate related to the day, week, month, or season. This would be an opportunity to introduce *Chase's Calendar of Events*, almanacs, or other library books that tell what is celebrated on specific days. You may also help students find Web sites with similar information. Allow students to choose from celebrations they have discovered. Hold a class vote to determine one. Write it on the board, newsprint, or overhead transparency for the class to see. Ask for a five-syllable line about your topic and write it under the title. Ask for a seven-syllable line, etc. When you have all the lines, revise together, making the poem as clear and concise as possible. Then count the syllables out loud together. Have the class read the poem in unison to celebrate this day.

Variations

- Have students work in groups of three or four, going through the same process as above.

- Help students use reference books or Web sites to identify unusual special days. Have groups of three to five students choose different days to celebrate. Collaborate with the social studies teacher to help with this. Assist groups in writing their tanka and creating a *PowerPoint* presentation, video, or audio presentation of their poem. (Computer lab technicians can also help with this.) Make these available in the library and on the school Web page for viewing or listening by all students.

- Ask the principal if your students can read their tanka over the intercom during daily announcements to celebrate a special day (or make a non-special day special).

- Special times to highlight:
  - National Book Week
  - National Children's Book Week
  - National Education Week
  - National Library Week
  - National Poetry Month (April)

∞Rhyme

Rhyme pleases the ear by putting together words with accented syllables, usually endings, that have the same vowel sound. Note that though rhymes sound the same, they are not always spelled the same. Most students' earliest exposure to rhyme is through songs and nursery rhymes. Rhyme provides comfort through its predictability, especially in songs and rhymes with a repeated refrain.

The rhyming activities below teach students another way of creative expression. They help students differentiate between how rhymes look and how they sound. They ask students to apply language techniques accurately.

The library media specialist can teach students how to use rhyming dictionaries and Web resources about rhyming.

Ask students what a rhyme is and how to make one. You can define "rhyme" as words that sound alike. Ask what words do not have rhyming words. ("Orange" is considered one.)

Hear a Rhyme
For grades K–2

 ***Materials needed:*** Selected poem

Supports AASL Information Literacy Standards 2, 3, 6, 9

Supports NCTE Standards 3, 6,11

Choose a nursery rhyme or Dr. Seuss book with strong, regular rhymes. After discussing rhyme, tell students that you will read a poem. They should listen for words that sound like (whatever the rhyming word is). When students hear it, they should put one hand on their heads. When you see hands on students' heads, stop and check their accuracy. Write the words on the board so students can see what the sounds look like. Then continue with the poem.

Next, read the poem again, with the same instructions. This time, read it through without stopping.

Rhyme Chime
Used in classroom.

 ***Materials needed:*** Chime or bell, board or overhead, writing tool, dictionary

Supports AASL Information Literacy Standards 2, 3, 5, 9

Supports NCTE Standards 6, 11, 12

Before this activity, the library media specialist will teach students how to read the pronunciation information given in dictionaries. He or she can also teach usage terms found in dictionaries, such as "slang" and "obsolete." This will prepare students for challenges and questions during the activity.

Do a simple rhyming exercise with the class. Choose a word with many rhymes, such as "at" and write it on the board or overhead. Have a musical chime or bell (The Rhyme Chime) near you, at The Rhyming Station. Students should stand and prepare to move by row toward The Rhyming Station. Each student takes a letter of the alphabet in succession. When each student reaches the station, he or she says the letter, then the rhyme. If the student thinks the rhyme is a real word, he or she rings the Rhyme Chime and continues to his or her seat. (Slang and names are fine, but have a dictionary ready to settle disputes.) You write the word on the board or overhead. The next student continues at The Rhyming Station with the next letter.

You will want to point out spelling and pronunciation differences. In this example, "e" will generate "eat," which is a word, but not a rhyme of "at."

If a student rings The Rhyme Chime, but his or her rhyme is not a real word, other students make a buzzing noise. (This encourages all students to listen.)

Then stop and discuss whether the rhyme is a word. Is there a way to make it a word by adding a syllable to the beginning of the word?

When you have gone through the alphabet, ask if you have left out any possible rhymes. The answer should be yes, because you have not included initial consonant blends. See what rhymes students can make using initial consonant blends, such as "bl," "br," "ch," "cl," etc.

Variation

For a simplified version of Rhyme Chime, do the activity without the chime. Have students remain in their seats and call out their rhyming word.

Extension: Primed for Rhyme

This is a follow-up activity to Rhyme Chime, or initial activity for students who have had practice rhyming.

Materials needed: Board, overhead, paper, writing tools, rhyming dictionaries, computer with online access to rhyming resources

Supports AASL Information Literacy Standards 1, 2, 3, 4, 5, 6, 9

Supports NCTE Standards 3, 5, 6, 8, 11, 12

Rhymes alone do not usually make a poem, because no message is communicated. To make a poem, ask the class to choose one of the words from Rhyme Chime as the end of the first line. Then have them come up with a line. For example, if they choose "hat," the line might be, "The man downstairs wears a funny hat." Pick another rhyme for the end of line two and a line to go with it that expands the idea of the first line. For example, "It looks just like a big orange cat." Continue to lines three and four. Voila! A rhyming poem is born.

Give students another word that is easy to rhyme, such as "sit." Have students use any available rhyming resources and write their own four-line rhyming poem.

Resources

Rhyming dictionaries, such as Sue Young's *Scholastic Rhyming Dictionary*, and Web sites will help students find rhyming words of more than one syllable. One such Web site is *Rhyme Zone.* 2002. Lycos.com. 5 Dec. 2002 <www.rhymezone.com>.

A Web site that teaches how to rhyme is Tucker, Bob. *Grandpa Tucker's Rhymes and Tales.* 2 Nov. 2002. 5 Dec. 2002 <www.night.net/tucker/>.

Computer Rhymes

Materials needed: Computer with online access, and word processing and graphics software; computer disks, printer, prepared computer folder as described below

Supports AASL Information Literacy Standards 1, 2, 3, 4, 5, 6, 8

Supports NCTE Standards 3, 5, 6, 8, 11, 12

Students can use word processing programs to write their own four-line rhyming poems. Make a folder called "Four Liners," with files containing easy-to-rhyme words. Students open the file and create poems, based on techniques above. Have them save the file to a folder with their own names or save to the original file, making sure they have put their name on their poems. Students may print and share their favorites by reading them to the class or displaying.

Software programs can help students organize rhyming words and ideas by using flow charts, bubbles, and other graphical organizers.

Resource
Scholastic. *Annie's Rhyme Time*. 2002. 5 Dec. 2002. <http://teacher.scholastic.com/annie/>. Play Annie's riddle game. Make rhymes to answer the riddles and submit them to the Web site.

Rhyme Scheme Detectives

Materials needed: Prepared list of rhyme schemes (see below for examples), copied for each student; examples of poems using various rhyme schemes on overhead or slide; library poetry books; computer with Web access

Supports AASL Information Literacy Standards 1, 2, 3, 5, 6, 8, 9

Supports NCTE Standards 1, 3, 6, 7, 8, 11, 12

This activity can be team-taught, with the classroom teacher beginning the lesson and explaining the assignment. The library media specialist then assists students in their search for poems.

Rhyme schemes demonstrate to students that language has various patterns. Students will apply language skills to recognize patterns in a wide range of poetry.

Show a Four Liner to the class, and explain that poems have various rhyming patterns called rhyme schemes. The first line is always labeled "A." Each new end-line sound is indicated by the next letter of the alphabet. In the case of the Four Liner poems, the rhyme scheme is AAAA. This is rare, though Tennyson's "The Eagle" (Hale 43) is AAA BBB.

Show students poems with different rhyme schemes, such as:

- limericks (AABBA) (Jackson).

- A poem with AABBCCDDEE rhyme is Ogden Nash's "The Adventures of Isabel" (Hale 180).

- An example of ABCB rhyme scheme is John Updike's "January" (Prelutsky Random 36).
- An example of ABAB rhyme scheme is Lewis Carroll's "The Crocodile," (Prelutsky Random 81).

When students understand the concept, explain that they are being hired as Rhyme Scheme Detectives. Rhyme schemes must be found, and the detectives must comb the area and bring them in.

Working in groups of three or four, students are given a list of rhyme schemes they must find. (Include the ones above; add others as desired.) Determine a date by which the detectives must give their report. Their mission is to use library poetry books or poetry Web sites to find rhyme schemes matching those on the list. Like good detectives, students must write down the evidence—title of the poem, book in which it was found, page number, or Web site address. (If you like, make a template for students to complete.) They should find as many as they can of each rhyme scheme listed.

On the due date, groups report their evidence. If possible, give prizes or privileges to groups with the most titles, one for each rhyme scheme, and most overall. Have them read samples of the poems they found.

Variation
Rhyme Scheme Detectives can also use computer files to keep their lists, with one folder per group and one file per rhyme scheme.

Pick a Poem

 Materials needed: One set of paper slips containing rhyme schemes, one containing vocabulary words; baskets to put the slips in

Supports AASL Information Literacy Standards 3, 5, 6, 9

Supports NCTE Standards 3, 5, 6, 11, 12

Have two baskets prepared. In one baskets, place slips of paper on which you have written a simple rhyme scheme. Rhyme schemes may be repeated, but you must have at least one slip per student. In the other basket, place words from the students' spelling or vocabulary lists. Words may be repeated, but you must have at least one slip per student. Have students come forward and draw one slip from each basket. Then have them write a four-line poem containing their word and rhyme scheme. They may work in pairs or individually. The library media specialist will help students find rhyming words by showing them rhyming dictionaries and appropriate Web sites, such as Rhyme Zone. 2002. Lycos.com. 5 Dec. 2002 <www.rhymezone.com> and Tucker, Bob. *Grandpa Tucker's Rhymes and Tales*. 2 Nov. 2002. 5 Dec. 2002 <www.night.net/tucker/>. When students are finished, volunteers may read their poems aloud.

Predict-a-Rhyme

 ***Materials needed:*** Selected poem

Supports AASL Information Literacy Standards 2, 3, 4, 5, 6, 9

Supports NCTE Standards 1, 2, 6, 11, 12

This activity and its extension help students apply contextual clues and language patterns to complete lines. It allows for creative expression, while promoting accuracy.

Choose a poem with rhyming words the students will know, but a poem with which they are probably not familiar. Some suggestions are:

- Robert Louis Stevenson's "My Shadow" (Stevenson 8)
- Edna St. Vincent Millay's "Afternoon on a Hill" (Hale 106)
- Hilaire Belloc's "Matilda Who Told Lies, and Was Burned to Death" (Hale 276)

Tell students you will read the poem, and when you stop, they should call out the rhyming word.

For example:

> Library media specialist or teacher:
>
> "I have a little shadow that goes in and out with me,
>
> And what can be the use of him is more than I can" Students: "SEE."
>
> Library media specialist or teacher:
>
> "He is very, very like me from the heels up to the head;
>
> And I see him jump before me, when I jump into my" Students: "BED."
>
> If students choose the wrong word, talk about context and poetic devices to help them understand why the poet chose the word he or she did.

Extension: Unpredictable Rhyme
Distribute copies of a poem (suggestions above) with rhyming words in parentheses (words that students would say, above). Next to the rhyming word, type a blank. Have students write other rhymes that could make sense. Have them read their finished products aloud.

Chapter 3   The Wonderful World of Words

The next building block of language is words. To understand the power that words can have, consider the impact of this one-word sentence: "Oh!" Choosing the right word for any given purpose is, as Mark Twain said, "The difference between lightning and the lightning bug" (Letter to George Bainton, October 15, 1888). Poetry is an especially appropriate vehicle for word study, because of its concise, vivid word choice. Applying poetic techniques to our use of language enhances communication.

During your study of words, you may like to read to your students Nancy Byrd Turner's poem, "Words" (Hale 210).

Word Choice

Using the perfect word in the perfect way gives language power. Students already know that one word can have several meanings and several words can have the same general meaning. Helping them learn when to use which word will develop their sense of appropriateness, style, and audience.

The activities below help students interpret and evaluate language and access information in a variety of ways.

Connotation Conundrum

 Materials needed: Dictionaries, slang dictionaries, books and online resources that list slang terms for certain time periods, copies of the Connotation Conundrum chart

Supports AASL Information Literacy Standards 1, 2, 3, 5, 7, 8, 9

Supports NCTE Standards 1, 3, 6, 7, 8, 9, 11, 12

This is another good team-teaching activity, with the library media specialist teaching students how to use a variety of print and Web resources and the classroom teacher teaching the content of the lesson.

A connotation is the association people make with certain words. Some connotations are societal, some are regional, and some change with time.

Challenge students to consider the language they use in contrast to the language their parents and grandparents use. Have available dictionaries, slang dictionaries, thesauri, and other reference books and Web sites. Photocopy the following chart and distribute it to students:

Good	Bad

Figure 3.1: Connotation Conundrum

Ask students what words or phrases they use to mean these words. (For example, "cool" is used to mean "good.") Have them write their words in the appropriate column. Then have students use slang dictionaries to find other words or phrases that mean these words. Students may also like to interview their parents and grandparents to collect more words or phrases. When students have 10 words or phrases in each column, have them use those words or phrases plus their own words to create a poem.

Resources

 Books:

Dictionaries, slang dictionaries, thesauri, and other sources of slang terms.

Garrison, Webb B. *What's in a Word: Fascinating Stories of more than 350 Everyday Words and Phrases,* Nashville, TN: Rutledge, 2000.

Scholastic Children's Dictionary, NY: Scholastic, 2002.

Terban, Marvin. *It Figures! Fun Figures of Speech,* NY: Clarion, 1993.

—. *Scholastic Dictionary of Idioms,* NY: Scholastic, 1998.

 Web Site:

Melanie and Mike. *Take Our Word for It.* 25 Nov. 2002. 5 Dec. 2002. <www.takeourword.com/theory.html>.

Wilton, David. *Wilton's Word and Phrase Origins.* 4 Sept. 2002. 5 Dec. 2002. <www.wordorigins.org>.

Variation: School slang dictionary

 Materials needed: Computer, word processing program, disks

Supports AASL Information Literacy Standards 1, 2, 3, 4, 5, 6, 7, 9

Supports NCTE Standards 4, 5, 6, 7, 8, 9, 11, 12

Students can create an on-going slang dictionary for the school. The library media specialist helps students create a computer file in a word processing program. The dictionary can be kept on a hard drive or disk in the library. Each entry should be alphabetical and follow a template similar to this:

Slang term

Meaning

Used in a sentence:

Students are often unaware they are using slang, so a discussion of slang versus standard English would be worthwhile. Have the class listen for their own slang usage and ask them for a standard English synonym.

Have them write two poems that have the same meaning, one that only students would understand and one that their parents or grandparents would understand. Have them test themselves by showing both poems to their parents or grandparents. Did they understand one and not the one written for students?

Extension: Translation Time

 ***Materials needed:*** School slang dictionary

Supports AASL Information Literacy Standards 1, 2, 3, 5, 6, 9

Supports NCTE Standards 3, 4, 5, 6, 7, 8, 9, 11, 12

The library media specialist helps students access the school slang dictionary and guides students toward the correct use of words. When at least a dozen words or phrases are collected in the school slang dictionary, have students each choose several and use them in their correct context in a poem. Have students exchange papers. The receiving student should write a "translation" of the poem, keeping the author's meaning, but using standard English. Hand papers back to the author and allow pairs to discuss the accuracy of the translation. Volunteers may share aloud with the class.

Extension: Old-Time Translation Time

 ***Materials needed:*** audiotape recorder (optional)

Supports AASL Standards 1, 2, 3, 4, 5, 6, 9

Supports NCTE Standards 1, 3, 4, 5, 6, 7, 8, 9, 11, 12

Have students interview their parents or grandparents about slang they used as children. They should take notes but may also use an audiotape recorder. The library media specialist can teach students to use the audiotape recorder and offer tips for good quality taping and interviewing, such as questioning techniques. Have students write poems using these slang terms. Then have them read and explain their poems to the class.

Matching Meanings

 ***Materials needed:*** Copies of a selected poem, with some of the words underlined; dictionaries (print or online)

Supports AASL Information Literacy Standards 1, 2, 3, 5, 6, 9

Supports NCTE Standards 3, 6, 8, 11, 12

Choose a poem containing words familiar to the students. Suggestions are:
- Shel Silverstein's "Sarah Cynthia Sylvia Stout Would not Take the Garbage Out"
- Elizabeth Coatsworth's "Swift Things are Beautiful"
- Jane Yolen's "Homework"
- Alfred Noyes' "Daddy Fell into the Pond" (Hale 196, 369, 124, 73, respectively).

This activity promotes the students' understanding that words have more than one meaning. Students also access and interpret information when finding dictionary entries.

The library media specialist can lead the entire activity or help students with their dictionary work, letting the classroom teacher lead the rest of the activity.

Type the poem, underlining some of the familiar words. Distribute to students. Working alone or in pairs, students will look up the underlined words in the dictionary and determine which meaning applies in each case. Have them write the number of the meaning above the word. Discuss the poems when students are finished. Ask if students learned any new meanings for familiar words.

~*Where Do Words Come From? Etymology and Word Meanings*

The activities that follow will increase students' awareness of words and their meanings, teach students how to read etymology information in dictionaries and find regions in atlases, and help students creatively express their new understandings of words.

In the Beginning
For grades 5–6

 Materials needed: Dictionary containing etymologies or copy of an entry from the *Oxford English Dictionary*, atlas

Supports AASL Information Literacy Standards 1, 2, 3, 5, 6

Supports NCTE Standards 1, 3, 6, 7, 8, 11, 12

The history of a word indicates its original meaning and shows whether it has changed through time. Show students how to read the etymology notes in dictionaries. (Though most children's dictionaries do not include etymologies,

Scholastic Children's Dictionary, does.) If possible, show them an entry from the Oxford English Dictionary. Choose a common word, such as nice, and follow the history from its beginning. Show students an atlas, so they can see from what part of the world the words came. (Collaborate with the classroom teacher or social studies teacher with this.) Are there any surprises about this word, either in the way it has been used or in who used it? Has the meaning changed? If so, are there clues about why?

Have students work alone or in pairs, looking up at least one word each (choose from vocabulary or spelling lists), filling out the chart on page 27.

In the Beginning
Etymology = Word History

Word: _____

First came from language: _____

Meaning: _____

Also came from language: _____

Meaning: _____

Also came from language: _____

Meaning: _____

What the word means now:

_____

_____

_____

Use the word in a sentence:

_____

_____

_____

Figure 3.2: In the Beginning

Extension: Etymology Poetry
Using the words from the etymology chart, have students write a poem about one of the words. The poem should use the word's origin and various meanings. Have volunteers read their poems when they are finished.

Etymology Forest
For grades 4–6

 **Materials needed:** Green, blue, and brown paper; markers; tape or tacks; dictionaries, other books about word origins, online resources.

Supports AASL Information Literacy Standards 1, 2, 3, 5, 6, 7, 9.

Supports NCTE Standards 1, 3, 6, 7, 8, 11, 12.

Prepare wall or bulletin board with green bottom for grass, blue top for sky. Cut out brown rectangles for tree trunks, smaller brown rectangles for tree roots, and long, thin rectangles for branches. Choose words from students' spelling or vocabulary lists. Put students in groups of four or five, and assign each group a word. With markers, they should write the word on the tree trunk. Using library and Web resources, the group then looks up the roots of the word (Old English, etc.) and writes them on the roots. Next, the group writes each meaning on a branch. Each group places the tree on the wall or bulletin board, creating a forest.

Variation: Etymology Tree
Instead of a forest, choose one word, and make one tree, with some students working on the roots and some working on the meanings.

Extension: The Fruitful Forest or Tree
Have students think about and discuss the words in the forest, their meanings, and roots. They may work either in groups or individually. Using what they have learned, have them write poems using the words or any part of the word's history or meaning. Then have students cut fruit shapes out of colored paper and use a marker to write their poems on their shapes. Then they may attach these to the tree.

After some work with words and their meanings, students will enjoy the word play in this anonymous poem (Hale 218):

HAVE YOU EVER SEEN?

Have you ever seen a sheet on a river bed?
Or a single hair from a hammer's head?
Has the foot of a mountain any toes?
And is there a pair of garden hose?

Does the needle ever wink its eye?
Why doesn't the wing of a building fly?

Can you tickle the ribs of a parasol?
Or open the trunk of a tree at all?

Are the teeth of a rake ever going to bite?
Have the hands of a clock any left or right?
Can the garden plot be deep and thick?
And what is the sound of a birch's bark?

Resources

 ### Books:

Various dictionaries and reference books, such as:

Garrison, Webb B. *What's in a Word: Fascinating Stories of more than 350 Everyday Words and Phrases,* Nashville, TN: Rutledge, 2000.

Scholastic Children's Dictionary, NY: Scholastic, 2002.

Terban, Marvin. *It Figures! Fun Figures of Speech,* NY: Clarion, 1993.

—. *Scholastic Dictionary of Idioms,* NY: Scholastic, 1998.

 ### Web Site:

Melanie and Mike. Take Our Word for It. 25 Nov. 2002. 5 Dec. 2002 <www.takeourword.com/theory.html>.

Oxford English Dictionary. 2002 Oxford U. 5 Dec. 2002. <www.oed.com/public/welcome/>. (Full access is subscription only, but parts are open to guests.)

Wilton, David. Wilton's Word and Phrase Origins. 4 Sept. 2002. 5 Dec. 2002 <www.wordorigins.org>.

✦ Alliteration

Alliteration is the repetition of consonant sounds, especially initial consonants, within a line. A moderate amount of alliteration sounds pleasant, but too much sounds forced and trite. The activities below reinforce students' understanding of consonant sounds and spelling. A couple of the activities give practice in word choice and allow students freedom to create.

Tongue Twisters

Tongue twisters offer a fun way to introduce students to alliteration. Some qualify as poetry because of their rhythm or rhyme. Here are two popular examples:

PETER PIPER

Peter Piper picked a peck of pickled peppers.
Did Peter Piper pick a peck of pickled peppers?
If Peter Piper picked a peck of pickled peppers,
Where's the peck of pickled peppers Peter Piper picked?

BETTY BOTTER

Betty Botter had some butter,
"But," she said, "this butter's bitter.
If I bake this bitter butter,
it would make my batter bitter.
But a bit of better butter—
That would make my batter better."

So she bought a bit of butter,
Better than her bitter butter,
And she baked it in her batter,
And the batter was not bitter.
So 'twas better Betty Botter
Bought a bit of better butter.

Morris Bishop's "Song of the Pop-Bottlers" and Carolyn Wells' "A Canner Exceedingly Canny" are other good examples. (Ferris 358, 364.)

Resources

 *Books*

Cole, Joanna, comp. *Six Sick Sheep: 101 Tongue Twisters*, NY: Scholastic, 1993.

Harrison, Michael and Christopher Stuart-Clark. *The Oxford Treasury of Children's Poems*, NY: Oxford U P, 1999.

Rosenbloom, Joseph and Mike Artell. *The Little Giant Book of Tongue Twisters*, NY: Sterling, 1999.

Rosenbloom. *World's Toughest Tongue Twisters*, NY: Sterling, 1987.

Seuss, Dr. *Oh Say Can You Say?* NY: Random, 1979.

Schwartz, Alvin. *Busy Buzzing Bumblebees and Other Tongue Twisters*, NY: Harper, 1982.

 Web Site:

Staley, C. T., ed. *Tongue Twister Database*. 1 July 2002. 5 Dec. 2002 <www.geocities.com/Athens/8136/tonguetwisters.html>.

Giggle Poetry. Meadowbrook Press. 5 Dec. 2002 <www.gigglepoetry.com/>. Poetry activities, contests, games, links to poets.

Battle of the Tongues

  Materials needed: timer, copies of tongue twisters

Supports AASL Information Literacy Standards 3, 5, 6, 7, 9

Supports NCTE Standards 3, 11, 12

This activity improves speaking and listening skills, in addition to reinforcing the concept of alliteration. Practice selected tongue twisters together as a class. Have students identify the alliteration. Is the same letter repeated, or the same sound? (For instance, is some alliteration created by the "c" and some by the "k"?) You may like half of the class to speak and half to listen. Then switch, so everyone has a chance to hear the effect of the alliteration. Say the tongue twisters slowly, and then increase speed.

    Then divide into groups of threes. The library media specialist or teacher sets the timer for one minute (or longer, depending on your students' abilities). One student will repeat the tongue twister until the timer sounds. The others act as judges. One judge keeps track of the number of times the speaker says the tongue twister. The other judge makes a mark on paper for each speaking error the speaker makes. Then the students rotate positions until all three have spoken.

    Scoring is as follows: Each team totals the number of times the tongue twister was said. Then total the number of errors. Then subtract that from the number of times the tongue twister was said. The highest number wins. If possible, provide prizes or privileges to the winners. You could also have one winner for the most times the tongue twister was said and another for fewest errors.

Rise and Fall
Caution: This is *not* a quiet activity

  Materials needed: Tongue twister projected on overhead transparency

For variations: Songs for all to see

Supports AASL Information Literacy Standards 2, 3, 5, 6, 9

Supports NCTE Standards 3, 11, 12

Review alliteration. Show students a tongue twister and have them identify which letter is alliterated. Have the class recite a tongue twister aloud together. All begin seated. When the alliterative letter is said, all stand. When the next alliterative letter is said, all sit, and so on until the end. Gradually increasing your speaking speed will add to the fun and make students think faster.

Variations

- Do **Rise and Fall** by singing an alliterative song, such as "Animal Fair," "Cotton-Eye Joe," "Li'l Liza Jane," or another song the students know (*American 6*, 28, 68, respectively). Project the words on an overhead transparency. Together, find the alliteration, and then choose the alliterated sound to which you will sit and stand. You may need to change sounds for different verses or lines. (Collaborate with the music teacher, if necessary.)

- Put students in groups and do **Rise and Fall** as a round, singing "Row, Row, Row Your Boat," "Three Blind Mice," or another alliterative round. Together, find the alliteration, and review where to sit and stand before beginning. Note: Students can help prepare this activity with help from the library media specialist by finding appropriate songs in the library, student music texts, or online.

Word Swap

 ***Materials needed:*** Typed, altered poem, as described below, one copy for each student and copy or projected image of the original poem

Supports AASL Information Literacy Standards 2, 3, 5, 9

Supports NCTE Standards 3, 5, 6, 11

This activity helps students use information accurately and creatively, and makes them apply knowledge of language structure and vocabulary.

Use an appropriate poem with strong alliteration. Examples, with one possible source given, are:

- Robert Southey's "The Cataract of Ladore" (Opie 94)
- Robert P. Tristram Coffin's "The Skunk" (Ferris 168)
- William Blake's "The Tiger" (Ferris 178)
- Alfred Tennyson's "The Brook" (Ferris 272) and "The Eagle" (Ferris 291)
- Rowena Bennet's "The Witch of Willowby Wood" (Hale 324),
- e.e. cummings' "Maggie and Milly and Molly and May" (Hale 139).

Type the poem, inserting a synonym for the alliterated word and underlining it. Ask students to think of a word that means the same thing as the underlined word, but begins with the initial letter of a preceding word. Have them read the lines both ways, asking them which sound they like better. For example:

Adapted from "The Tiger" by William Blake

> Tiger! Feline! burning light,
> In the forests of the night,
> What immortal hand or eye
> Could frame thy dreadful symmetry?

Then show the original, and have students compare the synonyms they chose with the poet's words.

Original verse from "The Tiger" by William Blake:

> Tiger! Tiger! burning bright,
> In the forests of the night,
> What immortal hand or eye
> Could frame thy fearful symmetry?

(Many editions use Blake's original spelling, "Tyger.")

～Assonance

Assonance is the repetition of vowel sounds within a line. It creates unity and sets a mood. A fun, anonymous example is:

> Moses supposes his toeses are roses,
> But Moses supposes erroneously;
> For nobody's toeses are posies of roses
> As Moses supposes his toeses to be.
> (Hale 205)

Other more standard examples are:
- Robert Louis Stevenson's "Travel" (Ferris 459)
- Elizabeth Barrett Browning's "How Do I Love Thee?" (Hale 144)
- Irene Rutherford McLeod's "Lone Dog" (Prelutsky 65)

- Eve Merriam's "What in the World?" (Prelutsky 114)
- Robert Southey's "The Cataract of Ladore" (Opie 94)

In the activities below, students will evaluate texts and accurately identify assonance. They will apply knowledge of language skills, such as pronunciation and spelling.

Color Code It

 ***Materials needed:*** Highlighters or markers, poems typed as described below

Supports AASL Information Literacy Standards 2, 3, 5, 6, 9

Supports NCTE Standards 3, 6, 11

Type poems that strongly demonstrate assonance and enlarge them so that one poem fills one page or give students examples of poems and have them do the word processing. After you have introduced the concept of assonance, distribute the poems. Have students use highlighters to color code the words or syllables with the same vowel sounds, one color for each sound. They may work alone or with a partner. When they are finished, ask for results. "What other words sound like 'X'?" You may also point out spelling differences for the same sound. Post the color-coded poems on the bulletin board or wall.

Variations

- Type poems that strongly demonstrate assonance and enlarge them so that one poem fills one page. Put students in groups of four or five, or have them work by rows. Assign a vowel sound found in the poem and color to each group. For example, group one has blue, which equals the long o sound. Ask the group to use only its color and mark only its vowel sound. When everyone is done, read the poem. Each group reads the words it marked. You read the in-between words.
- Vary this activity by making it similar to **Rise and Fall**. Each group stands and sits when its sound is read aloud.

Vowel Speak

 ***Materials needed:*** Selected poem, overhead or slide

Supports AASL Information Literacy Standards 2, 3, 5, 6, 9

Supports NCTE Standards 1, 3, 6, 11, 12

Choose a poem with strong assonance (suggestions above). Project it on an overhead transparency or *PowerPoint* slide. Identify the assonance. Recite the poem together. Talk about what effect the assonance has on the poem's meaning and mood. Then recite it saying the vowel sounds only. How does it sound?

∽Onomatopoeia

Onomatopoeia is a word or words that sound like the thing it is naming, for example, "buzz." Awareness of onomatopoeia adds richness to students' vocabulary. It helps students think descriptively and listen carefully.

Introduce onomatopoeia with examples such as Edgar Allan Poe's "The Bells" (Ferris 64), David McCord's "Song of the Train" (Ferris 188), William Shakespeare's "Song: Hark, Hark!" (Perrine 200). Ask the class to identify onomatopoeia. Then have them think of common words that are really onomatopoeia. Examples are "clap," "thunder," and "roar."

Name that Sound
Used in classroom.

 Materials needed: Sound effects tape or audio CD

Supports AASL Information Literacy Standards 1, 2, 3, 4, 5, 6, 9

Supports NCTE Standards 4, 5, 6, 8, 11, 12

In preparation for this activity, the library media specialist can teach students how to find sounds on the Internet and download them legally to an audio CD or computer file. He or she can help students make a tape or audio CD of sounds they create themselves. A sound effects tape could also be used. Five to 10 sounds are needed for this activity.

When it is time to begin, students should have paper and pencil ready. Play the sound. Have students write the word the sound is making, creating their own onomatopoeia. They should work on their own, without discussion. You may have to play each sound more than once. When the students have written their words, ask them to use those words (and others, if needed) to write a poem. Then have students read the finished poem to the class.

In conjunction with this activity, the library media specialist can read to students from Katz.

Variation

Have each student or group of students make a sound for the rest of the class to name. When the students have written their words, ask them to use those words to write a poem. Then have students read the finished poem to the class.

Resource

Book:

Katz, Bobbi. *A Rumpus of Rhymes*, NY: Dutton, 2001.

∽Diamante

Used in classroom.

 ***Materials needed:*** board or overhead, writing tool

Supports AASL Information Literacy Standards 1, 3, 5, 6, 9

Supports NCTE Standards 3, 6, 11, 12

The diamante form takes its name from its diamond shape, with its seven lines centered on the page. Each line is a prescribed part of speech. If students have not yet learned parts of speech, teach it if they are ready. If they are not ready, describe the words needed. If they have learned parts of speech, writing in this form reinforces their lessons.

Writing diamantes requires planning ahead, as the traditional form consists of antonyms in lines 1 and 7 and descriptive words about those nouns. Explain that antonyms are words that mean the opposite of each other. The library media specialist can help teach opposites, help students identify opposites, and read aloud Richard Wilbur's poem, "Opposites" (Hale 353).

The form is:

Line 1   One noun, an antonym or contrast to Line 7

Line 2   Two adjectives that describe Line 1

Line 3   Three gerunds (verbs with –ing endings) that relate to Line 1

Line 4   Four nouns, the first two relate to Line 1, the second two relate to Line 7

Line 5   Three gerunds that relate to Line 7

Line 6   Two adjectives that describe Line 7

Line 7   One noun, an antonym or contrast to Line 1

A sample:

light

bright, yellow

glowing, shining, warming

morning, afternoon, evening, night

creeping, blanketing, sleeping

quiet, black

dark

Introduce diamante form and write a diamante poem together as a class before beginning activities.

Batter Up!

 Materials needed: Diamante templates

Supports AASL Information Literacy Standards 3, 5, 6, 9

Supports NCTE Standards 5, 6, 11, 12

The library media specialist teaches students how to identify parts of speech in the dictionary and helps students understand the different meanings for the same word.

Put students in groups of six. Give them copies of Figure 3.3, the Diamante Template. Explain that each student in each group is a batter (with pencil as bat). You will throw out the first pitch (the first word). (Be sure to choose a noun that has an obvious antonym or contrast.) A student writes that on his or her group's paper. From there, they must score hits (write the poem), passing the paper from one to the other. Each person in the group finishes a line. If a player cannot finish a line, he or she strikes out and passes the paper to the next player. When the group finishes, the runner (one player from the group) goes to home base (a designated place, such as the front of the room) with the complete poem. When all the groups are finished, the runners recite their groups' poems.

_____
(noun)

_____, _____
(two adjectives describing Line 1)

_____ing, _____ing, _____ing
(three verbs relating to Line 1)

_____, _____, _____, _____
(two nouns relating to Line 1,
two nouns relating to Line 7)

_____ing, _____ing, _____ing
(three verbs relating to Line 7)

_____, _____
(two adjectives describing Line 7)

_____
(noun, antonym or contrast to Line 1)

Figure 3.3: Diamante Template

Variation: Run the Bases
Same as above, but have three or four "pitches" (Line 1 words) for each group already written on the templates. Distribute the first pitch paper, and proceed as above. The runner then comes to you for the second pitch, etc. When groups have done three or four, have them choose their favorite to recite to the class.

Computer Baseball

Materials needed: Prepared computer files or disks, as described below; computer disks; computers with word processing or graphics software; printer

Supports AASL Information Literacy Standards 1, 3, 5, 9

Supports NCTE Standards 1, 3, 5, 6, 8, 11, 12

Both **Batter Up!** and **Run the Bases** can be played in word processing programs. The library media specialist can teach students how to use the hardware and software. Collaborate with your computer lab technician if necessary. Prepare one computer disk for each group of six students. Put the Diamante Template, Figure 3.3, on the disk, with your "first pitch" (the first word) on the first line. (Be sure to choose a noun that has an obvious antonym or contrast.) For **Run the Bases**, put several templates with first lines on a disk. From there, each group takes its disk to the computer where students take turns "facing the batter" or "running the bases." Have students save their poems, printing out the best one to recite to the class.

Reflection poems
Used in classroom.

Materials needed: Diamante shape worksheets

Supports AASL Information Literacy Standards 3, 5, 6, 9

Supports NCTE Standards 5, 6, 11, 12

Show that diamante poems are really two halves of a diamond. Each half is the opposite of the other in meaning. Introduce or review the term "antonym," and how and where to find an antonym. The library media specialist can teach students how to find antonyms in dictionaries and thesauri.

Distribute paper to each student with this form drawn on it:

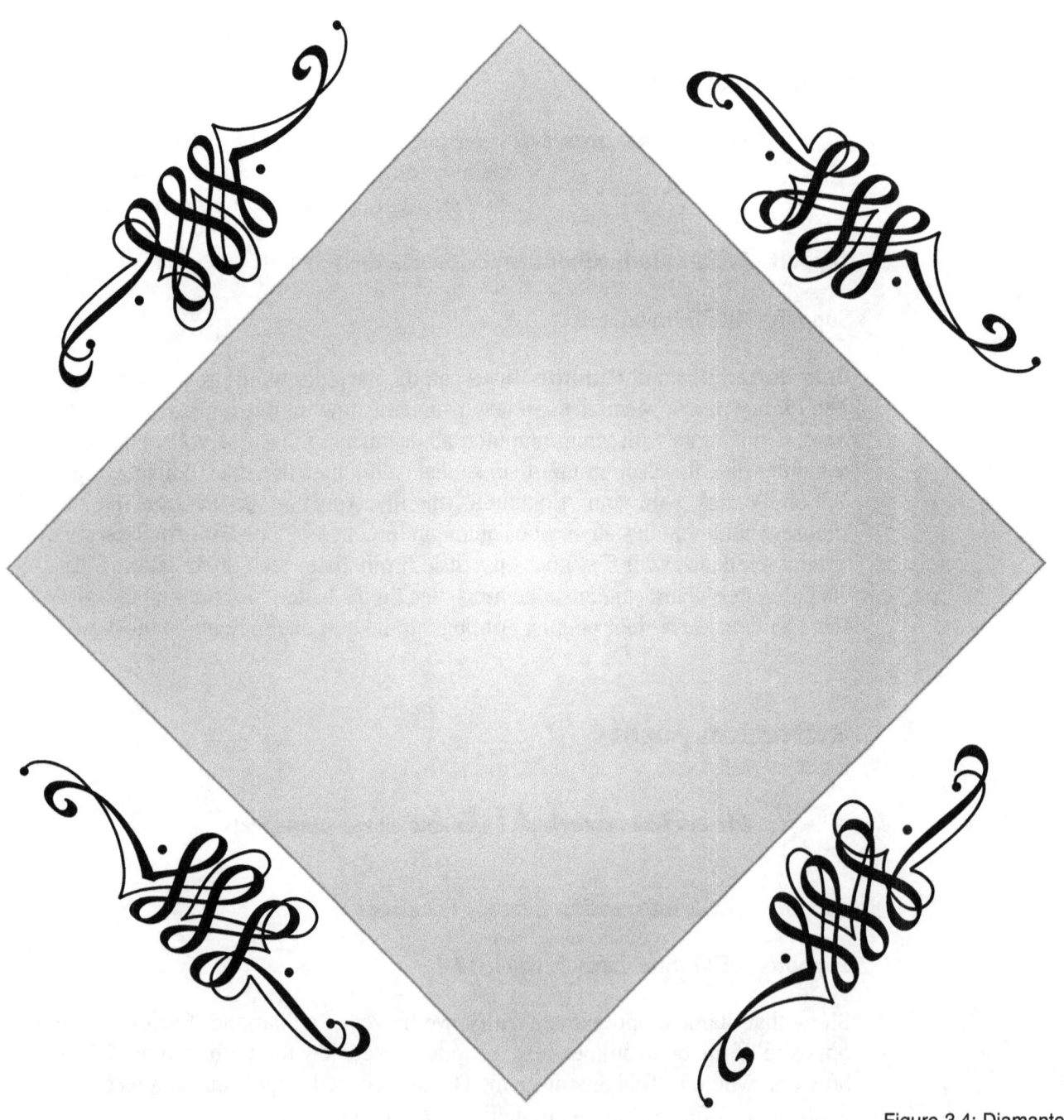

Figure 3.4: Diamante

Have each student use diamante form to write the first half of the poem. (You may want to insert lines for students to follow.) Then have everyone pass their papers to the right and complete the poems they have received. Hand them back to the originators, so everyone can see how the poem turned out.

Diamond Graphics

Materials needed: Poems, computer with word processing and graphics software, art supplies, printer

Supports AASL Information Literacy Standards 1, 2, 3, 4, 5, 6, 9

Supports NCTE Standards 5, 6, 8, 11, 12

Have groups take their favorite diamante poems, eliminate underlines and description, and decorate them. The library media specialist can help students do this with a computer graphics program, geometry software, art supplies such as markers, glue, and glitter, or all of the above. Collaborate with your math teacher for shape reinforcement lessons. Hang students' creations in a visible place, or post them to the school Web page.

Go Fly a Diamante!

Materials needed: card stock, wire, ribbon or yarn, markers, student diamante poems

Supports AASL Information Literacy Standards 3, 5, 6, 9

Supports NCTE Standards 5, 6, 11, 12

Have students use markers to write their diamante poems on diamond-shaped colored cardstock. Attach wire to one point. Make a tail from bows of ribbon or yarn. The library media specialist can give students decorating ideas by helping them find books and Web resources with pictures of kites.

Sponsor a "Diamante Flying" session in the school yard, with students reading their poems as they "fly." Invite the principal and other special guests. This would be especially appropriate during April, National Poetry Month.

Variation
Make diamante "kites" as above, but attach to bulletin board with sky blue background. Have students decorate the ground and add birds and clouds to the sky.

Resources

Web Site:

Ramsey, Inez. *Forms of Poetry for Children*. James Madison U. 5 Dec. 2002 <http://falcon.jmu.edu/~ramseyil/poeform.htm>.

Diamante Structure. School District of Siren, Siren, WI. 5 Dec. 2002. <www.siren.k12.wi.us/hs/academics/Englishrocks/English%2011/poetry-diamante.html>.

~Style

Style is the way a piece of writing is written. This general term includes word, grammar, and mood choice. Certain writing styles appeal to some audiences more than others, depending upon their age, education level, gender, personalities, and interests. Style may be labeled colloquial, playful, sophisticated, informal, formal, and many other adjectives.

Awareness of style will help students learn about language's effects and appropriate use for various audiences.

Grammar Matters

Materials needed: Selected poems, worksheets.

Supports AASL Information Literacy Standards 2, 3, 5, 6

Supports NCTE Standards 1, 3, 6, 9, 11

Choose two or three poems that have deliberately bad grammar or non-standard English, such as:

- Ben King's "That Cat" (Hale 20)
- James Whitcomb Riley's "Little Orphant Annie" (Opie 300)
- Shel Silverstein's "Valentine" (Prelutsky 38)
- Langston Hughes' "Mother to Son" (Hale 97).

Give each student one worksheet for each poem. Read the poems aloud and have students fill in their worksheets. Discuss their answers when they are finished. You might also like to project the words of the poems on an overhead transparency, so students can see the dialect spelled.

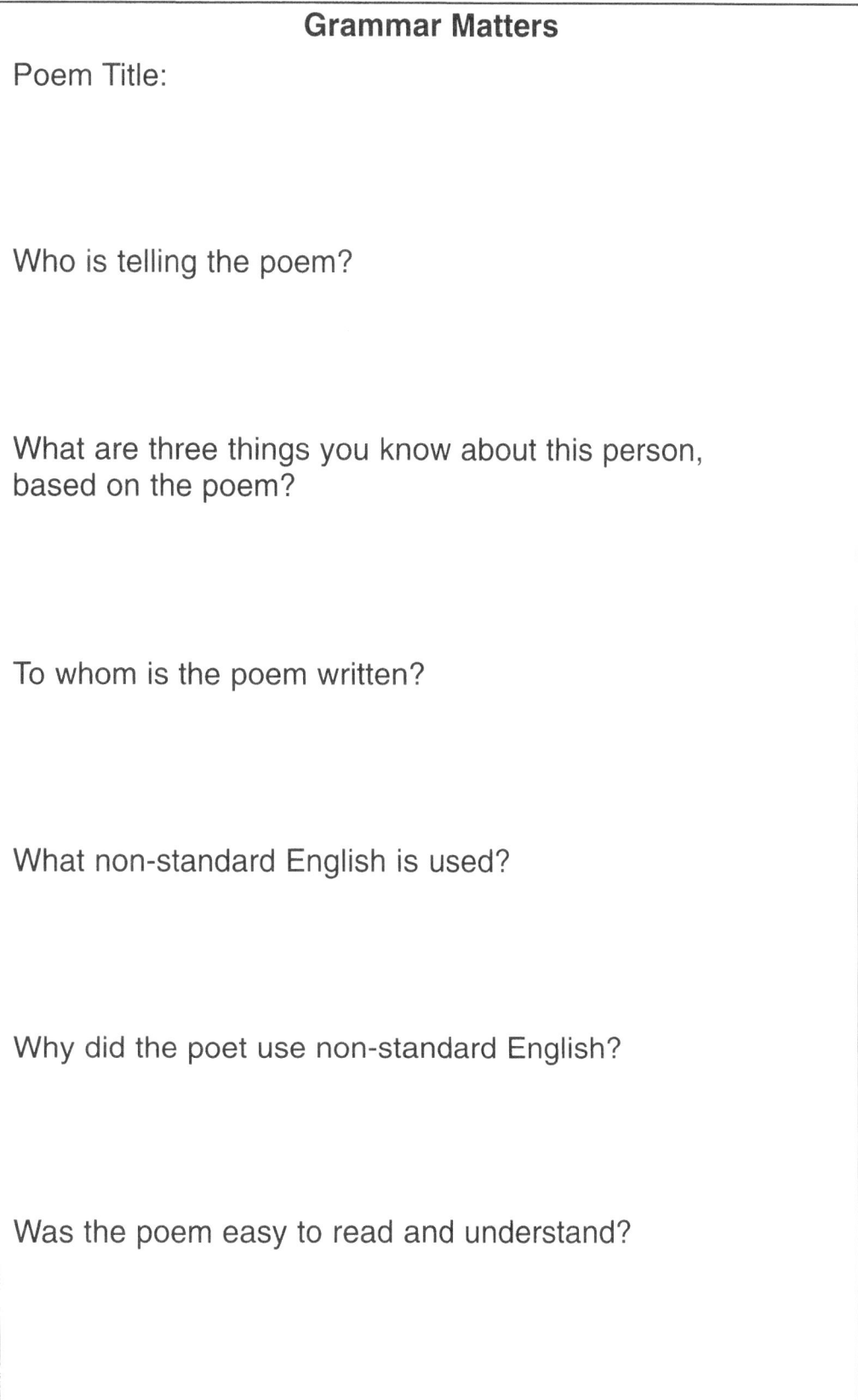

Figure 3.5: Grammar Matters

Extension: Who Said It?

 ***Materials needed:*** Selected poems, worksheets, computers with word processing and graphics software, general art supplies

Supports AASL Information Literacy Standards 2,3, 5, 6, 9

Supports NCTE Standards 1, 3, 6, 8, 9, 11, 12

Use 8½" × 11" paper, turned "Landscape" orientation, with the 11-inch sides as top and bottom. Have students type poems (suggestions under **Grammar Matters**) in a word processing program or print by hand on one half of the paper. On the other side, have them decorate the poem by depicting the poem's narrator. They may create computer-generated artwork or use traditional art methods. The library media specialist can teach students how to use hardware and software in collaboration with the computer technician and art teacher. Post the poems and artwork on a bulletin board or wall or on your school Web page.

Style Awhile

 ***Materials needed:*** Selected poems, projection method

Supports AASL Information Literacy Standards 2, 3, 4, 5, 6

Supports NCTE Standards 1, 3, 5, 6, 9, 12

Choose three poems written in different styles about one subject (animals, food, people, etc.). Many anthologies are arranged by topic to simplify selection.

Suggestions for friendship are:

- Langston Hughes' "Poem" ("I loved my friend …") (Hale 141)
- e.e. cummings' "In Just-" (Ferris 73)
- Rabindranath Tagore's "Gift" (Pinsky 265)
- Robert Louis Stevenson's "Pirate Story" (Stevenson 53).

Suggestions for cats are:

- T.S. Eliot's "Macavity: the Mystery Cat" or "Song of the Jellicles," (Opie 346, 347–8)
- Ben King's "That Cat" (Hale 20)
- William Wordsworth's "The Kitten at Play" (Ferris 157)
- William Carlos Williams' "Poem" ("As the cat …)" (Ferris 159).

Ask students to jot down a few words about the topic—anything that comes to mind as important about the topic. Now show them (using overhead projector or *PowerPoint* slides) the first poem. Read it once or twice. Ask students what they notice about the way the poem was written. Have them point out poetic devices they have learned, such as alliteration, etc. Does it rhyme? What is its rhythm? Does it use long or short words? Familiar or unfamiliar words? What is the poet trying to tell about the topic? Does the way it was written match the poem's message? How would students describe the mood of the poem? Continue to the next poem, and the next. Then show all three poems, if possible. Ask students, "Which poem more closely fits your ideas about the topic, based on the words you wrote?" Point out that one topic can be treated in widely different ways in poetry.

Now have students write their own poem about the topic, based on the words they have written down. If they like, they may imitate the style of the poem they preferred. Have students read their poems aloud or type them into a library computer file for others to read.

Extension

Students have written one poem about a topic. Now have them write another poem about the same topic, but in a different style. They may imitate the style of another of the poems you discussed.

Variation: Computer Style

 Materials needed: Selected poems, prepared in computer file; computer and word processing software

Supports AASL Information Literacy Standards 2, 3, 4, 5, 6, 8

Supports NCTE Standards 1, 3, 5, 6, 8, 9, 12

Style Awhile can be done using computer software, such as Kidspiration®, or by making a file in a word processing program. The file will contain the poems and questions, and students can save their work in files under their names. The library media specialist will teach students how to use hardware and software to complete the activity.

The Fashion Runway

 Materials needed: Magazines or catalogs to cut up, scissors, glue sticks

Supports AASL Information Literacy Standards 1, 2, 3, 5, 6, 9

Supports NCTE Standards 1, 2, 3, 6, 11, 12

In preparation for this activity, the library media specialist will collaborate with the classroom teacher to find appropriate poems, as described below. The library media specialist can also assist groups as they work on the activity.

For the activity, divide students into groups of four or five. Have prepared poems of a variety of styles, two per group. Give each group different poems. Use poets from James Whitcomb Riley to Shakespeare and anyone in between. Each poem should take half of the page.

To help students understand the difference between colloquial, informal, and formal English, have them think about style in terms of clothing. First, talk about the difference between work clothes (or play clothes), school clothes, and dress-up clothes.

Have magazines or catalogs available. Distribute poems to groups, one poem per group at one time. The groups' instructions are to read the poem and decide what style it is. If it were a person, how would it dress? Jeans and a T-shirt, formal gown? Students should cut pictures from magazines or catalogs and "dress" the poem according to its style. Students should use a glue stick to put the pictures on the page beside the poem. When they are finished with one, they may get another poem and continue.

Conclude the activity with groups walking down a fashion runway. (If the library is appropriately configured, the fashion walk could be held there.) Each group "models" its poem in front of the class by reading it, describing the clothing they selected, and telling why. You or other students may disagree with their choice. If so, those who disagree must give reasons for their opinions.

Variations

Instead of fashion, have students match the poems to musical type. Would the poem be rap, rock, easy listening, jazz, country, or classical? The library media specialist in collaboration with the music teacher can teach students how to find and listen to a variety of music online as examples.

Materials needed: Computer with word processing and graphics software, computer file containing selected poems and appropriate graphics and music.

Supports AASL Information Literacy Standards 1, 2, 3, 4, 5, 6, 8, 9

Supports NCTE Standards 1, 3, 5, 6, 8, 9, 12

Either the fashion or music activity could be done by individuals or groups on the computer by creating a file containing the poems and having students match them to pictures of clothing or legally downloaded music that represents a music type. The library media specialist will assist students in their hardware and software instruction, as well as teaching copyright basics as they apply.

Chapter 4 A Turn of Phrase

Words work together in groups to create images and express thoughts. "Now and then I come across a passage, perhaps only a phrase, which has a meaning for me, and it becomes part of me" (W. Somerset Maugham). A clever turn of phrase surprises readers and helps them remember the poem.

Imagery uses phrases to paint a picture in readers' minds. It can illustrate an abstract quality by describing concrete things. One form of poetry is even called "Concrete"! Imagery can describe a familiar thing so that the thing becomes new.

Imagery is often achieved with metaphor and simile. A metaphor creates a stronger image than a simile, because a metaphor says that something is something else. A simile says something is like something else. The more the things being compared are dissimilar, the greater the surprise of the poem.

The activities in this chapter will have students apply language knowledge accurately and creatively. They will identify, interpret, and create comparisons. They will use a variety of print and online resources to access information.

Observe, Describe

 Materials needed: Selected poem on overhead transparency, overhead projector, ordinary object as described below

Supports AASL Information Literacy Standards 2, 3, 5, 6, 9

Supports NCTE Standards 1, 3, 6, 11, 12

Use a poem that describes something familiar to students. Some suggestions are:
- "The Snake" by Emily Dickinson
- "On the Porch" by Donald Justice
- "My Mother's Hands" by Anna Hempstead Branch
- "The Snowflake" by Walter de la Mare
- "Night Stuff" by Carl Sandburg
- "Sea Shell" by Amy Lowell (Hale 52, 85, 99, 224, 251, 365, respectively).

Project the poem on an overhead transparency and read it aloud. Ask students if their experience with the subject matches the poet's. Were there any surprises in the poem? Any phrases they especially liked or disliked? What details were used in describing the item?

Next, choose an ordinary item and ask students to describe it (a book, a chair, a notebook, a pencil, etc.). Write their responses on the board or on an overhead projector transparency. Then write a class poem using the words and phrases listed.

This activity could be team-taught, with the library media specialist choosing and reading the poem and leading the discussion. The language arts teacher could complete the lesson.

Variation: The Match Game

 ***Materials needed:*** Ordinary objects as described below

Supports AASL Information Literacy Standards 1, 2, 3, 5, 6, 9

Supports NCTE Standards 3, 4, 5, 6, 11, 12

Give each student a similar, but different item (a stone or a button, for example). If done in the library, the library media specialist could connect this with a display of a collection of some kind. Use the collection pieces as the item to give to students. Or use similar-looking books as the item.

Have students each write a poem describing their item. When they are finished, put all the items on a desk or table (or back in the collection display area). Then have a student read his or her poem. The other students should be able to guess which item was his or hers. Continue until all are matched.

Variation: Hand Me Downs

Supports AASL Information Literacy Standards 2, 3, 5, 9

Supports NCTE Standards 4, 5, 6, 11, 12

The library media specialist finds appropriate poems about hands or fingers and reads one aloud to the class. "My Mother's Hands" by Anna Hempstead Branch is one example (Hale 99). Either the library media specialist or the language arts teacher teaches the rest of the activity. Ask students to write poems describing their own hands. Encourage them to use metaphors, similes, and other poetic devices they have learned. Volunteers can read theirs for the class.

~Concrete Poetry

Concrete poetry is written to form a shape, usually of the thing the poem is about. Paul Janeczko's *A Poke in the I* is a book of concrete poems. Other concrete poems are:

- Shel Silverstein's "Poem on the Neck of a Running Giraffe" (*Where*, 107)
- James Stevenson's "Mystery" (32)
- A.B. Ross' "Two in Bed" (Ferris, 40)
- William Jay Smith's "Seal" (Prelutsky, *Random,* 62).

Show students examples of concrete poetry. Ask how the shape emphasizes the meaning of the poem.

Concrete ABC
For grades K–2

 Materials needed: old catalogs, magazines, and calendars; scissors; glue sticks; poster board

Supports AASL Information Literacy Standards 1, 2, 3, 5, 6

Supports NCTE Standards 3, 5, 6, 12

This activity will reinforce letters' shapes and help students connect the alphabet with initial letters of objects.

After showing examples of concrete poetry to students, have them each choose a letter of the alphabet. Have them write their letters on poster board, taking up most of the space. Then have students look in old magazines, catalogs, and calendars for pictures of things that begin with their letter. They should cut them out and use glue sticks to glue the picture to the outline of their letter. They should continue until the outline is covered with pictures.

When everyone is finished, they should hold up their letter and identify the items. Have students sign their creations and display them.

Poetry Room

 Materials needed: Large paper, tape or adhesive

Supports AASL Information Literacy Standards 1, 3, 4, 5, 9

Supports NCTE Standards 4, 5, 6, 11, 12

This activity would be especially suitable for a day in April, National Poetry Month. Have students work in pairs. Each pair should choose an object in the library or classroom to decorate with poetry—a table leg, table top, section of floor, light fixture (check with your fire marshal to do this safely), book shelf, chair back—anything is fair game. Each pair will measure the area and cut paper to fit the size and shape. Collaborate with your math teacher to help explain and supervise the measuring. Then each pair will design a poem about the object they are decorating. They will attach the poem with tape or another non-destructive fixative.

Extensions

- Ask the principal if someone from the class can advertise their Poetry Room creations over the school intercom.
- Have the Poetry Room on display for a special event, such as Parent-Teacher Conferences, or have a special open house. Have students available to give "tours" of their poems.

- Have students take close-up pictures of the Poetry Room and load them onto the school Web page. Have students put the pictures in a book to keep in the library.

Really Concrete Poetry
Used in classroom (or outside).

 **Materials needed:** Plaster of Paris, plaster cast forms or aluminum pans in various shapes

Supports AASL Information Literacy Standards 3, 5, 9

Supports NCTE Standards 4, 5, 6, 11, 12

Begin this activity with the library media specialist showing students examples of concrete poetry. Discuss how the shape and meaning go together.
   Collaborate with your art teacher to create real concrete poetry. Use plaster of Paris and ready-made forms available at craft stores or aluminum pans in various shapes. Have students work in pairs. Each pair should choose a shape and write a concrete poem in that shape and size. Mix the plaster of Paris and have students write their poem and signatures in it before it sets. Allow it to dry, and you have concrete poetry!

Extensions

- Collaborate with your science teacher and use library and Web resources to learn about plaster of Paris and how it works.
- Have students decorate their poetry by adding marbles, twigs, stones, etc. if it enhances their poem.
- Put the finished plaster pieces in the lawn at school or display in the library.

Metaphor

Color Me Poetry
For grades K–2

 **Materials needed:** *Hailstones and Halibut Bones* by Mary O'Neill, many sheets or pieces of paper per student of each color mentioned in the book

Supports AASL Information Literacy Standards 2, 3, 5, 6, 9

Supports NCTE Standards 3, 5, 6, 11, 12

Choose two or three poems to read and colors to emphasize. Lay colored paper where students can pick it up when directed. Ask students to pick a piece of paper the color of (one of the things mentioned in the poem). Have students hold up the color they chose. Ask why they chose that color. Continue for two or three rounds. Then read the selected poem to the class. Have them hold up their color when the color name is mentioned. Point out that sometimes we compare a thing to something else so we can understand it in a new way.

Extension

Have students "write" their own color poems by drawing or using pictures from old catalogs and magazines. Help them print any necessary words. Have them recite their poems to the class and display them when they are finished.

Variation: Color My Senses

Choose a color from the book *Hailstones and Halibut Bones* by Mary O'Neill. Ask students what the chosen color smells like, tastes like, feels like, looks like, and sounds like. Then read the poem. Ask if students agree or disagree with the poet's description. Point out that although we know that a color does not really have a smell or sound, thinking of a color in this way helps us understand it differently.

Extension

Have students make posters of a color's smell. Label the top of the poster board "Blue Smells Like," for example. Have students draw illustrations or find pictures in old magazines or catalogs to affix to the poster board.

Using the images on the poster board, the class dictates a poem to the library media specialist or teacher.

Display the poem and illustration.

Weather or Not

 Materials needed: Copy of "Fog"

Supports AASL Information Literacy Standards 1, 2, 3, 5, 6, 9

Supports NCTE Standards 1, 2, 3, 4, 5, 6, 7, 8, 11, 12

Collaborate with your science teacher and have students look up information about fog. They may work individually or in pairs. Use library resources such as encyclopedias, books about weather, newspaper reports, and the Internet. Have them complete the following worksheet:

Weather or Not

Fog

1. What does fog look like?

2. How is fog created?

3. Where is fog most likely to occur?

4. What are the effects of fog?

5. List three words that describe fog.

Figure 4.1: Weather or Not

Use Carl Sandburg's much-anthologized poem, "Fog" (Hale 236) to demonstrate the power of metaphor. Read the poem to students, more than once if necessary. Ask, "What is the poet comparing the fog to?" "What words or phrases make you think of a cat?" "How is fog like a cat?"

Discuss the difference between the prose information on fog and the poem. What is the purpose behind each? Which helps students "feel" the fog better?

Now write the poem on the board or project it on an overhead transparency. Divide the class into groups of three or four. Each group will act out the poem. The students will become the fog/cat. Each group presents its interpretation to the class.

Next, give students another weather word (snow, hail, sleet, sun, etc.). Using "Fog" as a model, students will write a poem comparing the weather word to an animal. They may work individually or in pairs. Have them recite their poems and act them out when they are finished.

Extensions

- Groups perform their poems for other classes or special events.
- Students use a computer graphics program to decorate their poems or Sandburg's "Fog." Display them.

Moonstruck

 Materials needed: Round cookies or crackers, copy of "The Moon's the North Wind's Cooky"

Supports AASL Information Literacy Standards 1, 2, 3, 5, 6, 9

Supports NCTE Standards 1, 2, 3, 6, 7, 8, 11, 12

Vachel Lindsay's "The Moon's the North Wind's Cooky" (Ferris 265) offers another metaphor connecting a child's world with science. Collaborate with your science teacher. Use library and Web resources and have students work individually or in pairs to find out what the phases of the moon are and what causes them.

Discuss students' findings. Give each student a cookie or round cracker with strict instructions not to eat it immediately. Ask students, "If the cookie or cracker is the moon, which phase is it?" (Full.) "Now bite off enough to make a 3-quarter moon." Have students give the scientific background. "Now bite off enough to make a half moon." Have students give the scientific background. "Now bite off enough to make a quarter moon." Have students give the scientific background. "Now a new moon." Have students give a scientific background.

Tell students that people use their imaginations to make up stories about how things could have happened. We can enjoy these stories for fun, as we understand the science behind it. Read the poem aloud. Then discuss how the moon is like a cookie. How is the poem scientifically correct? How is it incorrect?

Extension: Out in Space

Supports AASL Information Literacy Standards 1, 2, 3, 5, 6, 9

Supports NCTE Standards 1, 3, 6, 8, 11, 12

Working in pairs in the library, the library media specialist helps students find other poems about the moon, stars, or planets (one poem per pair). Have them complete this worksheet, using library and Web resources to answer the questions:

Out in Space

Write the poem here:

What comparisons are used?

How are the things being compared alike?

What is scientifically correct?

What is scientifically incorrect?

Figure 4.2: Out in Space

Chapter 4: A Turn of Phrase

Discuss when all are finished.

Pop, Pop, Pop

 ***Materials needed:*** Popcorn, copy of "A Pop Corn Song"

Supports AASL Information Literacy Standards 1, 2, 3, 5, 6, 9

Supports NCTE Standards 1, 3, 4, 5, 6, 7, 8, 11, 12

Use Nancy Byrd Turner's "A Pop Corn Song" (Ferris 45). Collaborate with your science teacher or life skills teacher. Have students work in pairs using library and Web resources to learn the following:

Pop, Pop, Pop

Where did popcorn come from?

_____
_____
_____
_____

What makes it pop?

_____
_____
_____
_____

One amazing fact about popcorn is:

_____
_____
_____
_____

One thing I like about popcorn is:

_____
_____
_____
_____

Figure 4.3: Pop, Pop, Pop

Depending on your school's facilities and policies, if possible have students watch popcorn pop. Show them the kernels before popping. What do the kernels look like? Have a student record responses. As it pops, what does it look like? Have a student record responses. When it's popped, what does it look like? Have a student record responses.

Distribute the popcorn among the students and allow them to eat it while you read the poem. Ask, "What are the comparisons?" "Did it look that way to you?" "If not, can you understand how the poet saw it?" "What's this last verse about?"

Review the words and phrases students gave while popping the corn. Have them write their own "Song of Popcorn" and recite when finished.

Extension

Pop extra popcorn and have students string it using needle and thread. Hang the string over a bulletin board or on the wall, and display students' popcorn poems beneath.

~Simile

A simile is similar to metaphor. It uses "like" or "as" to make its comparisons, as in "My Love is Like a Red Red Rose" by Robert Burns (Hale 142). Other examples of poems with strong similes are:

- Emily Dickinson's "The Storm" (Hale 236) and "There Is No Frigate" (Hale 346)
- William Wordsworth's "The Daffodils" (Hale 242)
- Ogden Nash's "The Panther" (Ferris 331)
- "I've Got an Incredible Headache" by Jack Prelutsky (Prelutsky *New* 46)
- James Stevenson's "The Dredge" (Stevenson 39).

It's Like This

*Materials needed:* Selected poems.

Supports AASL Information Literacy Standards 2, 3, 4, 5, 6, 9

Supports NCTE Standards 3, 4, 5, 6, 8, 11, 12

Choose several poems with strong similes and read them aloud to students. Identify what is like what. How does the comparison fit? How does this comparison help us see the thing in a new way? As with metaphors, the more dissimilar the things being compared, the more surprising the poem.

Distribute this worksheet and have students complete it individually:

It's Like This

Today is like
_____
_____
_____

This season is like
_____
_____
_____

School is like
_____
_____
_____

My family is like
_____
_____
_____

My pet is like
_____
_____
_____

My town is like
_____
_____
_____

My favorite day of the week is _____, because it is like
_____
_____
_____

Figure 4.4: It's Like This

Have students think about what they wrote. Have them choose the one they like best and write a poem using the comparison they created. Students will recite them to the class when they are finished.

This activity could be team-taught, with the library media specialist reading the poems and leading the comparison discussion. The language arts teacher could complete the activity.

Extensions

- Students will post their poems to the school Web page, or a read-only file on school computers to share with other students.

- Collaborate with your art teacher. Using computer graphics and other art techniques, students create artwork depicting the comparison in their poem. Display.

I Am

Supports AASL Information Literacy Standards 1, 2, 3, 4, 5, 6, 9

Supports NCTE Standards 1, 2, 3, 4, 5, 6, 7, 8, 11, 12

Collaborate with your social studies or science teacher. If students are studying animals of the rain forest, for example, help them find resources about these animals. When they have learned some facts about various animals, ask them which one they are most like and why. Then have them write a poem about it that begins "I am like (name of animal)." Other units appropriate for this activity are modes of transportation, food, plants, planets, etc. Have students recite their poems to the class.

Extensions

Use the same extensions for this activity as for **It's Like This**, above.

Like, As, Is

 ***Materials needed:*** Selected poems on overhead transparency, overhead projector

Supports AASL Information Literacy Standards 2, 3, 4, 5, 6, 9

Supports NCTE Standards 3, 4, 6, 11, 12

Elementary students may not need to be able to define metaphor and simile. However, an awareness of the impact of language improves students' reading, writing, and oral language skills. One way to help students see and feel this impact is to compare poems, one using simile and one using metaphor. Consider, for example, these two: "Dreams" by Langston Hughes (Prelutsky 225) and "Dreams" by Cecil Frances Alexander (Hale 315).

Begin by reading the poems aloud and projecting the words on overhead transparencies. Ask students to identify the simile and metaphor. The style of the poems is very different, contributing to the poet's intended impact. Talk about other differences between the two poems. Which do students prefer and why?

Variation

Do the same activity as **Like, As, Is,** using two Langston Hughes poems, "Dreams" (Prelutsky, 225) and "Harlem: A Dream Deferred" (Grimes). The message and style are similar, but one uses metaphor, and the other uses simile.

Extension

Ask students to write their own "Dreams" poems about goals they hope to achieve. Encourage the use of metaphor and simile. When they are finished, have students exchange papers and underline the metaphors and similes they find. Then the authors should work in pairs and comment on each other's poems. These can also be recited in class, displayed, or typed into a word processing file.

Personification

Personification is a figure of speech that gives human characteristics to non-human things. "The sky wept," referring to rain, is a clichéd example. "Personification speaks to the sensitivity and capacity for empathy we often find in children, particularly those between the ages of eight and ten, and gives these feelings a natural outlet" (Armour 68).

The Bug in Teacher's Coffee and Other School Poems by Kalli Dakos contains poems written as if they were told by items in a school, such as a pencil, goldfish, and math test. Other examples of personification are:

- "The Butterfly's Day" by Emily Dickinsonn (Hale 45)
- "Wind" by James Stevenson (Stevenson 45)
- "The Sloth" by Theodore Roethke (Hale 32)
- "Laughing Song" by William Blake (Hale 134)
- "The Snowflake" by Walter de la Mare (Hale 224)
- "April Rain Song" by Langston Hughes (Hale 231)
- "Sea Shell" by Amy Lowell (Hale 365)
- "The Cloud" by Percy Bysshe Shelley (Ferris 76)
- "A Microscopic Topic" by Jack Prelutksy (Prelutsky New 100)
- "The Pan and the Potatoes" by Kirsi Kunnas (Berry 78).

In Living Color
For grades K–2

 **Materials needed:** "The Colors live" from *Hailstones and Halibut Bones* by Mary O'Neill, 59; pieces of colored paper for each student

Supports AASL Information Literacy Standards 2, 3, 5, 9

Supports NCTE Standards 3, 4, 6, 11, 12

Tell students that sometimes we describe things as if they were people, able to do and feel the things humans can. Have them listen for the human traits the poet has given colors in "The Colors live." Ask for responses after the poem is read.

Have each student choose a piece of colored paper. Then ask them, "How would your color dance?" Have them think for a moment before demonstrating to the class. Ask, "What kind of song would your color sing?" Have them think a moment before demonstrating. Continue with the other personifications in the poem.

Personification Improvisation

 **Materials needed:** Selected poem on overhead transparency, overhead projector

Supports AASL Information Literacy Standards 2, 3, 5, 6, 9

Supports NCTE Standards 3, 4, 6, 11, 12

Choose a poem with strong personification. Project the words using an overhead projector. Read the poem and identify the personification. Then together decide on actions that match the poem. Read the poem together, adding the actions.

Extension
"Perform" your poem for another class or special event.

Picture This

 **Materials needed:** Pictures of non-human things as described below

Supports AASL Information Literacy Standards 1, 2, 3, 4, 5, 6, 9

Supports NCTE Standards 4, 6, 8, 11, 12

Find a few pictures of non-human things and either post around the room or project on a screen using *PowerPoint* slides. The library media specialist can help students find appropriate pictures in books or online. Trees and animals are especially good subjects for this activity. Have each student choose one of the pictures and write a poem about the thing as if it were human. Display the poems with the appropriate picture.

Extension

Collaborate with your science teacher. Using library and Web resources, help students find facts about their non-human things. Have them take notes on their findings. Based on what they know now, would they change anything in their poems?

If I Were a ...

 Materials needed: Kalli Dakos' poems, slips of paper with classroom items as described below

Supports AASL Information Literacy Standards 2, 3, 4, 5, 6, 9

Supports NCTE Standards 3, 4, 5, 6, 8, 11

Use Kalli Dakos' school poems as examples. (*The Bug in the Teacher's Coffee and Other School Poems* is one of her books.) Read several or have students read several aloud. Before class time, write the names of library, classroom, and school items on slips of paper (pencil sharpener, globe, desk, table, etc.). Have each student draw a slip of paper. Have students write a poem as if they were that item. When they are finished, have them read their poem aloud without saying what the item is. Other students should guess the item. In a good poem, the item will be identified easily.

This activity could be team-taught, with the library media specialist finding and reading the poems and the language arts teacher completing the activity.

Extensions

- Display poems.
- Have students go to Kalli Dakos' home page <www.kallidakos.com>, sign her guest book, and send her their poems or comments. (The library media specialist or classroom teacher may want to read students' comments before they are sent.)

~Repetition

Repeated lines and phrases in language, called a refrain, help us learn the poem, song, or saying. "Brains are built to discern patterns and to make sense of what impinges upon them" (McCracken 7). Repetition offers students a life-line to the larger poem, song, or story, giving them confidence as they learn to read. They may not remember what animal the farmer takes next, but they can chime in on "Hi, ho, the dairy-o, the farmer in the dell."

Suggestions for poems with refrains are:

- A.A. Milne's "Buckingham Palace," "Happiness," "Puppy and I," and "At the Zoo" (Milne *When* 4, 6, 8, 48, respectively)
- Shel Silverstein's "Upstairs," "Peanut-Butter Sandwich," "Lazy Jane," and "The Bagpipe who Didn't Say No," (Silverstein *Where* 60, 84, 87, 132, respectively)
- Robert Frost's "The Pasture" (Hale 136)
- e e cummings' "Chanson Innocente" (also called "in Just-") (Ferris 73)
- Gabriela Mistral's "Rocking" (Berry 31)
- Grace Nichols' "Sea Timeless Song" (Berry 28)
- Vachel Lindsay's "The Potatoes' Dance" (Ferris 234).

I've Told You a Thousand Times

 ***Materials needed:*** Copies of selected poems

Supports AASL Information Literacy Standards 1, 2, 3, 5, 6, 9

Supports NCTE Standards 1, 3, 4, 5, 6, 8, 11, 12

Read a poem with a refrain, encouraging students to join in on the repeated lines. Define "refrain."

Ask students, "When a teacher or parents tells you to do something over and over, how do you feel?" ("Nagged" or "You know they mean it" are two likely answers.) Say, "Let's look at some poems to see why a poet uses a refrain." Put students in groups of three or four. Distribute copies of selected poems, giving each group a different poem. (This exposes students to more poems and more effects of refrain.) Have students complete the following form:

I've Told You

Name of poem:
_____
_____
_____

Poet:
_____
_____
_____

Repeated line or phrase:
_____
_____
_____

We think the poet repeated this line or phrase because:
_____
_____
_____

If the repeated line or phrase is not identical every time, why do you think the poet changed it?
_____
_____
_____

Did you like the repetition? Why or why not?
_____
_____
_____

Figure 4.5: I've Told You

(Note to library media specialist and teacher: To help students finish the statement "We think the poet repeated this line or phrase because," guide students toward answers such as "to emphasize a point," "to show he or she really means what he or she says," "to help us remember," etc.)

When students are finished, they will read their poems aloud to the class and tell the results of their group work.

This activity could be team-taught, with the library media specialist introducing the activity, reading the poem, encouraging participation, and defining "refrain." The classroom teacher could continue.

Variation

Post poems with refrains and accompanying questions in a library computer word processing file. Students read and answer the questions, saving their work in their own file or on disk. The library media specialist will assist students with the assignment, including hardware and software use.

Specify a due date. (This allows all students the opportunity to read and think about each poem.) On the due date, students bring printouts of their responses. The library media specialist or teacher directs students to take turns reading the poems, and leads everyone in discussion.

Echo

Materials needed: Selected poems on overhead transparency, overhead projector, ordinary object as described below

Supports AASL Information Literacy Standards 1, 2, 3, 5, 6, 9

Supports NCTE Standards 1, 3, 4, 6, 8, 11

Collaborate with the science teacher. Have students use library and Web resources to learn what an echo is. (You could also collaborate with your language arts teacher by having students use library and Web resources to learn the story of Echo in Greek mythology.)

Choose one or two poems with refrains. Project the words on an overhead transparency. Read the poems together. Now divide the class into halves, with one half being the "main voice" and the other half being the "echo," the repeating phrase. Read the poems again, this time with the repeated lines read as echoes.

Extensions

- Audio tape the above. Read enough poems to fill the tape and keep it in the library for others to hear. To avoid copyright infringement, use poems in the public domain or original student poems.

- Ask the principal if the class can read a poem performed as above on the school intercom.

- Perform your poem for other classes or special events.

Potato Puppets

Materials needed: Potatoes, copy of "The Potatoes' Dance," art supplies

Supports AASL Information Literacy Standards 1, 2, 3, 5, 6, 9

Supports NCTE Standards 3, 6, 8, 11

Read Vachel Lindsay's "The Potatoes' Dance" (Ferris 234) aloud to the class. Collaborate with your art teacher to create potato puppets. Give students potatoes, matchsticks, and art supplies. Use matchsticks as eyes and legs, as the poem suggests. Have students decorate the potatoes to look like people. Then have them act out the poem as it is being read, holding their potato puppets.

Extensions

- Make a puppet theater by setting a large box on a table with the bottom facing the audience. Cut out the top two-thirds of the box bottom to create a stage. Students may draw theater curtains on the box. Perform potato puppet shows for younger students and special events. (Students can add a cricket, leaves, and other effects, too.)

- Have students create a computer-animated version of the potato dance. Have it available in a computer file for others to view. Collaborate with your computer technician for assistance.

Variation

Do the above, but instead of real potatoes, have students cut potato shapes out of brown construction paper and decorate.

Raining Refrains

Materials needed: Large paper "umbrellas," narrow blue paper, markers

Supports AASL Information Literacy Standards 1, 2, 3, 4, 5, 6, 9

Supports NCTE Standards 2, 6, 8, 11, 12

Using library and Web resources, students work in groups of three or four to choose a poem with a refrain. Collaborate with the art teacher. Have students cut out paper to look like umbrellas and long, narrow blue rectangles to be used as rain. Students will use markers to write the main part of the poem on the umbrellas and the refrain on the "rain." One line of "rain" will be used for each refrain line. Display on the wall or bulletin board labeled "It's Raining Refrains!"

Figure 4.6: It's Raining Refrains!

Chorus

A chorus differs from a refrain in that a chorus is a whole stanza repeated throughout the poem. This is often seen in ballads, folksongs, and popular songs. Often these songs tell a story, and the chorus separates the "scenes." This will be covered in more detail in Chapter Five.

~Rhythm

Rhythm is the flow of sound. In music, rhythm is what we call "the beat." In speech, it refers to the rise and fall of accented and unaccented syllables throughout a phrase.

Poets refer to rhythm as meter. Meter is measured in feet, with one foot equaling one set of accented and unaccented syllables. This sounds more difficult than it is, as the reader naturally adapts the poem's rhythm because of where the accents fall.

The four main kinds of feet are:

- iamb (unaccented, accented)
- trochee (accented, unaccented)
- anapest (unaccented, unaccented, accented)
- dactyl (accented, unaccented, unaccented)

A line of poetry is measured by the number of feet it contains. For example, three trochees in a line are called trochaic trimeter. The most common meter and line is iambic pentameter, five sets of unaccented, accented syllables. It most closely resembles natural English speech. Shakespeare used it almost exclusively. Blank verse, a favorite form of Robert Frost's, is defined as unrhymed iambic pentameter. Elementary students probably do not need to know this. They should, however, be aware of "the beat" and notice that a poem has a pattern of beats whether or not the poem rhymes. In writing their own poems, they should understand that a regular rhythm pattern produces a pleasing effect. (See Perrine for more details about rhythm and meter.)

The activities about rhythm help students use information accurately and creatively, help them apply knowledge of language structure, and help them appreciate texts.

I Got Rhythm

 Materials needed: Selected songs and poems on overhead transparency, overhead projector, rhythm instruments

Supports AASL Information Literacy Standards 3, 5, 6, 9

Supports NCTE Standards 3, 6, 11

Collaborate with the music teacher and select several songs the students know. "This Land is Your Land" and "Yankee Doodle" are two examples (Cohn 370, 62, respectively). You could also collaborate with the social studies teacher to teach students songs related to the unit they are studying. Sing the songs, clapping along to the beat. Add rhythm instruments if possible.

Now try clapping and playing to poetry. Choose poems with a strong beat. Poems by Jack Prelutsky, Shel Silverstein, and Dr. Seuss are well-suited for this. Project the words on an overhead transparency. Everyone reads, claps, and plays together.

Extension: Poetry Band
Practice some of your poems with rhythm instruments, refining what instruments play where. When you are ready, your Poetry Band can play for other classes and special events.

Jump!

 Materials needed: Jump ropes, selected poems with words on overhead transparency, overhead projector

Supports AASL Information Literacy Standards 1, 2, 3, 5, 6, 9

Supports NCTE Standards 1, 3, 11, 12

Jump rope rhymes came into being to help keep the rhythm for the jumper and those turning the rope. Collaborate with your physical education teacher to work on jumping and rhythm. If you have room in the library, try it! Otherwise, go to the gym or outside.

Here are some sample jump rope rhymes:

> Blackbirds, blackbirds,
> Sitting on a wire.
> What do you do there?
> May we inquire?
> We just sit to see the day,
> Then we flock and fly away.
> By 1, 2, 3... .
>
> Bubble gum, bubble gum, chew and blow,
> Bubble gum, bubble gum, scrape your toe,
> Bubble gum, bubble gum, tastes so sweet,
> Get that bubble gum off your feet!
>
> I asked my mother for fifty cents
> To see the elephant jump the fence.
> He jumped so high he touched the sky,
> And never came back till the Fourth of July
> (Jump higher and higher)

When students are able to coordinate jumping and rhyming, have them jump to a poem with strong rhythm. Poems by Jack Prelutsky, Shel Silverstein (especially see "Jumping Rope" *Where* 62), and Dr. Seuss are well-suited for this. Project the words on an overhead transparency so all can read aloud, or have half the students read and half jump and then alternate.

Variation
Have students jump up and down or clap instead of jumping rope.

Extension
After students demonstrate an understanding of rhythm from **Jump!**, try **Jump!** or its variation with poems of subtler rhythm. Suggestions are:

- "Stopping by Woods on a Snowy Evening" by Robert Frost (Ferris 67)
- "I Hear America Singing" by Walt Whitman (Ferris 451)
- "Arithmetic" by Carl Sandburg (Prelutsky *Random* 218).

Read the chosen poem through before jumping. Project the words on an overhead transparency, so students can follow along. Point out that, although you are exaggerating the accented syllables, all language has rhythm.

Rap It Up

 Materials needed: Audiotape of rap beat

Supports AASL Information Literacy Standards 3, 4, 5, 6, 9

Supports NCTE Standards 4, 5, 6, 11, 12

Students are familiar with rap music, which depends on its beat and heavy bass. Collaborate with your music teacher to find a rap beat background (such as those found on electronic keyboards) or play instrumental music with a rap beat. (The band, DC Talk, is one example.) Play it for students and say nonsense words (da-da-DUM or tra-la-LA, for example) to the beat. Keep the beat playing and have students write their own rap about something they are studying. Have students perform their raps when they are done.

Extensions

- Have students perform their raps for other classes or special events.
- Ask the principal if students can read their raps over the school intercom during announcements. Or have students write an announcement in rap form.
- Assist students in posting audio versions of their raps on the school Web page or computer file.

Chapter 5 I Think I Can, I Think I Can: Thoughts

The purpose of language is to communicate. Words, phrases, and sentences are arranged in ways that mean something. Sometimes these are stories with characters, setting, and plot, beginning, middle, and end. Forms include newspaper reports, textbook chapters, novels, and poems. Helping students decipher phrases to gain comprehension is of utmost importance.

Because poems can convey short stories with a simple plot line and a few characters, poetry can be used to teach basic story elements and enhance reading comprehension.

The activities in this chapter help students apply and synthesize language knowledge, appreciate texts, use information accurately and creatively, and adjust their use of language for various audiences and purposes.

~Nursery Rhymes

For grades 4–6

 Materials needed: Selected nursery rhyme, copies of Nursery Rhyme template

Supports AASL Information Literacy Standards 1, 2, 3, 5, 6, 9

Supports NCTE Standards 3, 6, 11, 12

Nursery rhymes may be the first form of poetry a student hears. Most nursery rhymes tell a story. Ask students which nursery rhymes they remember. Choose one or two to examine more closely. "Jack and Jill," "Jack Sprat," and "Little Bo-Peep" are suggestions printed here:

> Jack and Jill went up the hill
> To fetch a pail of water.
> Jack fell down and broke his crown
> And Jill came tumbling after.
>
> Jack Sprat could eat no fat,
> His wife could eat no lean,
> And so between the two of them,
> They licked the platter clean.
>
> Little Bo-Peep has lost her sheep,
> And can't tell where to find them.
> Leave them alone, and they'll come home,
> Wagging their tails behind them.

Have students work in pairs to complete the following worksheet. You will type the nursery rhyme of your choice on top.

Nursery Rhyme

1. Who are the main characters?
   _____
   _____
   _____

2. Where does the action take place?
   _____
   _____
   _____

3. What is the main character's problem or problems?
   _____
   _____
   _____

4. Is the problem solved? If so, how? If not, what happens?
   _____
   _____
   _____

Figure 5.1: Nursery Rhyme

When students are finished, discuss their answers. Explain that stories have characters with a problem (or conflict) that is solved somehow. Nursery rhymes tell their stories with strong rhythm and rhyme.

Extensions

- The library media specialist can direct students to books and Web sites containing nursery rhymes. Students may work individually or in pairs. Have students choose their favorite nursery rhyme. Have them re-write the rhyme as a narrative story. Read aloud to the class. Have the class guess to which rhyme the story refers.

- Begin as above, but have students re-write the rhyme as if it were happening today in their neighborhood.

~Extra, Extra!

 Materials needed: Sample news story, computer with word processing program

Supports AASL Information Literacy Standards 1, 2, 3, 5, 6, 9

Supports NCTE Standards 1, 2, 3, 4, 5, 6, 11

Have students work in pairs. Using library and Web resources, they should choose a nursery rhyme and write it as a news story. Provide a sample news story from your local paper (or local paper's Web page) as an example. News stories contain facts and often have quotes by the people involved. News stories include who, what, when, where, why, and how.

When students are finished, they should hand in their stories. Choose two or three students to be newspaper editors. With assistance from the library media specialist, computer technician, and language arts teacher, they will create a newspaper from the class stories. Print enough copies for everyone in the class and post the newspaper to the school Web page for others to enjoy.

~Teaching Tales

For grades 4–6

Supports AASL Information Literacy Standards 3, 5, 6, 9

Supports NCTE Standards 3, 4, 11, 12

Collaborate with a kindergarten teacher. The library media specialist will assist students and teacher in finding nursery rhyme books and Web sites. Have the class help teach nursery rhymes to younger students.

~Teaching Tales II

**Materials needed:** *You Read to Me, I'll Read to You* by John Ciardi (You may want to have more than one copy.)

Supports AASL Information Literacy Standards 3, 4, 5, 6, 9

Supports NCTE Standards 1, 3, 4, 11, 12

Collaborate with classroom teachers to assist in developing this activity. Pair older students with younger ones. For example, pair a fourth-grader with a kindergartener. Have the students read to each other using John Ciardi's *You Read to Me, I'll Read to You.* Students may follow the books' directions, with older students reading the poems printed in blue, and younger students reading the poems printed in black. Students may read to each other line by line. Students may like a poem so much they both want to read it, either separately or in unison. Have the pairs talk to each other about what they liked or did not like about the poems they read. Have them keep a log of the poems they read and the date. Continue this activity over a period of time so that students develop rapport and feel comfortable reading aloud to each other.

As a conclusion to the activity, the library could sponsor a "Read to Me" event. Pairs would read their favorite poems aloud to a larger group.

Variation

Use nursery rhyme books or simple poetry books instead of Ciardi's book to do the same activity.

~Word Order, Anyone?

**Materials needed:** Copies of "Anyone Lived in a Pretty How Town"

Supports AASL Information Literacy Standards 1, 2, 3, 5, 6, 9

Supports NCTE Standards 3, 5, 6, 11, 12

Word order affects meaning, which, in turn, affects the thoughts conveyed. English uses certain patterns. Readers expect certain parts of speech to be in certain places. A simple sentence usually begins with the subject, a noun. Next comes the predicate, a verb, as in "She went."

Putting words in unusual order gives readers a surprise. The piece is harder to read and understand, but may give readers more to think about.

Divide students into groups of four or five. Project the words of "Anyone Lived in a Pretty How Town" by e e cummings (Hale, 292) on an overhead transparency. Read the poem once together. Students will immediately notice the unusual word order, which affects meaning.

76 Rhymes and Reasons: Librarians and Teachers Using Poetry to Foster Literacy

Give each group a typed copy of the poem. Have students cut the words apart, one verse at a time. Have them rearrange the words so that each verse and the poem as a whole make sense. They may leave words out, but they may not add any. They should tape the words onto a piece of paper. Have groups compare their poem with the original. Have groups read their resulting poems to the class. Which do students like best? Why?

Variations

- Have groups of three or four students create poems with Magnetic Poetry® Kids' Kit (available from <www.magpo.com> and elsewhere). Have them write down and recite their favorites to the class.

- Have groups of three or four students create their own poems by choosing words from the Magnetic Poetry® Web site, <www.magpo.com>. (Click "Play online," "Kids Kit.") Have them copy their best poems into a shared computer file for others to read.

- Cut 8½" × 11" sheets of paper in half. On each, write a spelling or vocabulary word. Include some prepositions and conjunctions. Put one word on the bulletin board or wall. Have students create a poem by taking turns choosing a word and adding to the poem. This can be a dynamic poem, as others make changes throughout the week.

ᴇ⁓Narrative Poems and Choruses

A narrative poem is one that tells a story. Some have choruses. A chorus is repetition, similar to a refrain. However, a chorus is identical lines repeated between verses. Many poems and songs have choruses, which listeners can easily learn, while the leader sings or says the verses.

The activities below have students read a wide range of poems from various time periods. They will apply language knowledge and interpret the poems accurately and creatively. They will evaluate information critically, adjust their use of language to communicate effectively with their audiences, and participate in groups effectively.

Musical Stories

 ***Materials needed:*** Selected song, book jackets with blurbs

Supports AASL Standards 1, 2, 3, 4, 5, 6, 9

Supports NCTE Standards 1, 2, 3, 4, 5, 6, 7, 8, 11, 12

Collaborate with your music teacher to find songs that tell a story. Some suggestions are:

- "Puff, the Magic Dragon" words by Lenny Lipton and music by Peter Yarrow (on Peter, Paul, and Mary's album *Peter Paul and Mommy*)
- "Going to the Zoo" by Tom Paxton (on Peter, Paul, and Mary's *Peter Paul and Mommy* album)
- "Sweet Betsy from Pike" (Cohn 186).

Words to some Peter, Paul, and Mary songs are also found on their Web site, <www.peterpaulandmary.com>.

Read the words of the chosen song together. Listen to it and sing along. Now have students write the story summary as if it were a book blurb (have them look at book jackets for examples) or a *TV Guide* description. Have students read them aloud.

Extension
Have students work in pairs. Each pair should use library and Web resources to choose a story poem or song. Then have them write a blurb summarizing the story. When all are finished, make overhead transparencies of each chosen poem. Project them on the overhead and have the class read them together. Then have each pair read their blurb, with the rest of the class matching the blurb to the correct poem or song.

Variation
Have students work in pairs. Each pair should use library and Web resources to choose a story poem or song. Then have them write a blurb summarizing the story. Have them type the poem or song lyrics into a computer word processing file called "Story Poems." Each poem should be numbered. Have them type their blurb in a different file called "Blurbs." Each blurb should be lettered. When all poems and blurbs have been keyed in, students should complete a worksheet you have created. It will look something like this:

> Match the story poem with its description.
>
> _____ 1. (Write in name of story poem)
>
> _____ 2. (Writing in name of story poem)
>
> and so on.

Post an answer key in the computer, so students can see their results.

Poetic History

 Materials needed: Selected poem on overhead transparency, overhead projector

Supports AASL Standards 1, 2, 3, 5, 6, 9

Supports NCTE Standards 1, 2, 3, 4, 5, 6, 7, 8, 11, 12

Many historical incidents have inspired poems. Collaborate with the social studies teacher, finding poems appropriate to the unit of study. Examples of historical poems are:

- "The Midnight Ride of Paul Revere" by Henry Wadsworth Longfellow (Hale 263)
- "O Captain! My Captain!" by Walt Whitman (Hale 156)
- "Charge of the Light Brigade" by Alfred, Lord Tennyson (Hale 270)
- "Nancy Hanks" by Rosemary and Stephen Vincent Benet (Ferris 438)
- "Barbara Frietchie" by John Greenleaf Whittier (Ferris 442)
- "The Erie Canal" (Cohn 116).

Choose an appropriate poem and project the words on an overhead transparency. Read it together. Then have students work in pairs to find other accounts of the same historic incident using library and Web resources. Assign one pair to learn about the poet and when and why the poem was written. Have groups report back to the class. Discuss the benefits and appropriate uses of the poem versus prose accounts and vice versa.

Variation
Poetic anything! Poems have been written about every subject. Use subject-appropriate poetry as a connection to students' units of study. Collaborate on the above activity with the appropriate teacher.

Extension
Have students write their own poems about an historic event. Have students read them aloud when they are finished.

Celebrate the Day

Supports AASL Standards 1, 2, 3, 5, 6, 9

Supports NCTE Standards 1, 2, 3, 6, 7, 8, 11, 12

Be as simple or elaborate as you like. Use *Chase's Calendar of Events* or another source that lists daily holidays. Find poems that match the day to share with students. For example, on National Pancake Day (February 12), read Jack

Prelutsky's "The Pancake Collector" (Hale, 190) and Shel Silverstein's "Pancake" (Silverstein *Where* 34). Listen to Carly Simon's song "Hotcakes" (from her album *Hotcakes*, Electra, CD released 1990). Have students write their own poems about pancakes. Students can use library and Web resources to find out more about National Pancake Day and look up recipes for pancakes and toppings. You could even serve pancakes, or make a batch together and eat them if you have access to a kitchen. If possible, collaborate with a classroom teacher (in this case, social studies or life skills) to make the day a real event.

Chart the Story

 ***Materials needed:*** Selected poem on overhead transparency, overhead projector

Supports AASL Standards 1, 2, 3, 4, 5, 6, 9

Supports NCTE Standards 1, 2, 3, 6, 8, 11, 12

Ask students, "What are the parts of a story?" They should be able to answer, "Beginning," "Middle," and "End." Then discuss what happens in each part. Usually, a story's beginning sets the scene and introduces the characters. The middle contains problems for the main character. The end resolves the problems. A story also has these elements: characters, plot (the action), setting (when and where it takes place), and theme (the main idea).

Choose a story poem and project the words on an overhead transparency. Read it aloud. Ask who the characters are, what the setting is, what the plot basics are, what the theme is. Then identify the beginning, the middle, and the end. Have students complete this chart:

Heitman

Figure 5.2: The Shape of a Story

Title of Poem:		
Beginning	Middle	End

- Characters (Name, Description)
- Setting (Where:, When:)
- Beginning Problem
- Problem gets worse
- Problem is worst
- Solution
- The End

Chapter 5: I Think I Can, I Think I Can: Thoughts 81

Draw lines connecting the boxes. This is the "shape" of a story.

Have students work in pairs, choosing their own story poem and charting it. Display on the bulletin board or wall when finished.

It's Story Time

 ***Materials needed:*** Variety of story poems

Supports AASL Standards 1, 2, 3, 4, 5, 6, 8, 9

Supports NCTE Standards 1, 2, 3, 4, 6, 8, 11, 12

Story poems lend themselves to recitation. Using library and Web resources, have each student choose a story poem he or she likes. Have them practice and then recite the poem to the class. (This can prepare students for the junior high and high school extra-curricular, oral interpretation.)

Extensions

- If the poem is in public domain, have students recite the poem on videotape and keep the tape in the library.

- Have students recite their poems for other classes or special events.

- If the poem is in public domain, collaborate with the computer technician to help students make an audio computer file. Have students type in words and add graphics. Post to the school Web page.

- Collaborate with the art teacher. Have students illustrate the poem, scene by scene. Have them print the poem's verses. Post verses and illustrations on the bulletin board or wall. Or have students create a mural depicting the story.

- Have students make their own books, either on paper or on the computer. Show them books of illustrated poems, such as *The Midnight Ride of Paul Revere* (Longfellow) and *Casey at the Bat* (Thayer). Collaborate with the art teacher and computer technician for assistance. Students may work in pairs or individually. They should choose a poem, decide on layout (which verses go where and what illustrations will accompany them), and create. When they are finished, display them.

In addition to story poems and songs given above, here are more story poem suggestions, with one source listed:

For younger students:
"The Duel" by Eugene Field (Ferris 349)

"Jest 'Fore Christmas" by Eugene Field (Ferris 538)

"The Monkeys and the Crocodile" by Laura E. Richards (Ferris 175)

"The Owl and the Pussycat" by Edward Lear (Ferris 354)

"Puppy and I" by A.A. Milne (Ferris 153)

For older students:
"Charge of the Light Brigade" by Alfred, Lord Tennyson (Hale 270)

"The Cremation of Sam McGee" by Robert Service (The Academy of American Poets <www.poets.org/Poems/>)

"Foul Shot" by Edwin A. Hoey (Prelutsky *Random* 220)

"The Highwayman" by Alfred Noyes (Hale 296)

"The Listeners" by Walter de la Mare (Ferris 513)

For everyone:
"The Adventures of Isabel" by Ogden Nash (Hale 180)

"Casey at the Bat" by Ernest Lawrence Thayer (Hale 260)

"The Creature in the Classroom" by Jack Prelutsky (Prelutsky *Random* 212)

"The Crocodile's Toothache" by Shel Silverstein (Silverstein *Where* 66)

"Daddy Fell into the Pond" by Alfred Noyes (Ferris 35)

"Little Orphant Annie" by James Whitcomb Riley (Ferris 532)

"Matilda who Told Lies, and was Burned to Death" by Hillaire Belloc (Hale 276)

"The Mungle and the Munn" by Jack Prelutsky (Prelutsky *New* 92)

"Paul Revere's Ride" by Henry Wadsworth Longfellow (Hale 263)

"The Spider and the Fly" by Mary Howitt (Hale 268)

"The Tale of Custard the Dragon" by Odgen Nash (Hale 172)

"The Walrus and the Carpenter" by Lewis Carroll (Ferris 328)

ᴖ*Dramatic Monologues*

Students may not need to know the term "dramatic monologue," but the form is interesting to examine. It helps students understand the story element "point of view." The poet may be writing as someone else. A dramatic monologue is a poem written to someone, with no reply from that someone. Examples are:
- "Time, You Old Gypsy Man" by Ralph Hodgson (Ferris 61)
- "Alas, Alack!" by Walter de la Mare (Ferris 132)

- "The Pasture" by Robert Frost (Ferris 230)
- "A Lesson for Mama" by Sydney Dayre (Hale 70)
- "Love" by William Jay Smith (Hale 141)
- "If" by Rudyard Kipling (Hale 356)
- "The Pancake Collector" by Jack Prelutsky (Hale 190)

Take a Letter

 *Materials needed:* Selected poem on overhead transparency, overhead projector

Supports AASL Standards 1, 2, 3, 5, 6, 9

Supports NCTE Standards 1, 2, 3, 4, 5, 6, 8, 11, 12

Choose a dramatic monologue poem. Project the words on an overhead transparency. Read the poem together and define any difficult words. Then have students write a letter to the poem's narrator, responding to the poet's comments or questions. Have students read their letters aloud when they are done.

Variations

- Post the poem in a computer file and have students respond in a computer word processing program, saving their work to a file in their name.
- If all students have e-mail, send the poem to them via e-mail and have them reply, copying all students so that everyone can see the responses.

Who's Who?

 *Materials needed:* Selected poems, art supplies

Supports AASL Standards 2, 3, 5, 6, 9

Supports NCTE Standards 3, 4, 6, 11, 12

The library media specialist will choose several appropriate dramatic monologue poems. Give students a copy of a dramatic monologue poem. (Use several different poems.) Collaborate with the art teacher and computer technician. Have students draw a picture or use a computer graphics program to create two visuals to accompany the poem. One visual should be of the narrator, and one should be of the person to whom the narrator is speaking. Post these with the poem for display.

Who Are These Guys?

 Materials needed: Copies of selected poem

Supports AASL Standards 2, 3, 5, 6, 9

Supports NCTE Standards 3, 4, 5, 6, 11, 12

The library media specialist will find an appropriate dramatic monologue poem. Project the words using an overhead transparency. Read it aloud. Then have half the class write a description of the poem's narrator. Have the other half of the class write a description of the person to whom the narrator is speaking. In both descriptions, have students include personality, looks, and any other traits they glean from the poem. When they are done, have students from the first half pair with students from the other half. Have them read their results aloud to each other. Then discuss results together as a class.

~Dramatization

 Materials needed: Selected poem, set and props as desired

Supports AASL Standards 1, 2, 3, 5, 6, 9

Supports NCTE Standards 1, 2, 3, 4, 6, 8, 11, 12

Dramatic poetry presentations have benefits for both the audience and the performers. "The truth about poetry is that it has an actual effect upon the listener. A great poem can make the hairs on your neck stand up" (Collom 212). For student performers, "Recent classroom-based research shows that language learning is enhanced when oral and written language experiences are interrelated" (Armour 89). Story poems are a natural for dramatic presentations. Dramatizations can be as simple or elaborate as you and your students care to make them.

Choral Reading

A simple vocal dramatization is done with choral reading. Choral reading involves the whole class, but it can feature parts, too. Prepared scripts are available (Scripts For Schools <www.scriptsforschools.com> is one source), but working out parts as a class helps students understand the meaning and mood of the poem. Alternate lines. Boys read, then girls, or vice versa. Decide together what should be spoken loudly or softly, quickly or slowly. Should the sound be high or low? You can easily write in parts on an overhead transparency that has the poem's words double-spaced. An example of choral reading directions follows. This poem was chosen for its excellent dramatic qualities, and it is in public domain. If you think this poem is not appropriate for your students, choose a different selection and follow the format suggested here.

> ### The Owl and the Pussycat (verse 1)
> *by Edward Lear*
>
> **Boys:** The Owl and the Pussycat went to sea
>
> **Girls:** In a beautiful pea-green boat:
> They took some honey,
>
> **Boys:** And plenty of money
> Wrapped up in a five-pound note.
>
> **Girls:** The Owl looked up to the stars above,
>
> **Boys:** And sang to a small guitar,
> "O lovely Pussy, O Pussy, my love,
>
> **Girls:** What a beautiful Pussy you are,
> You are
>
> **Boys:** You are!
>
> **All:** What a beautiful Pussy you are!"

You can change the room's atmosphere by turning off the lights for a scary poem, flashing them for stormy poems, etc.

Paul Fleischman's *Joyful Noise* and *I am Phoenix* are not technically "story poems," but two poetry books meant to be read "as a duet." Effective with two voices, it is easily adapted to more voices divided into two parts. Fleischman's *Big Talk* contains poems for four voices, with color-coded instructions for who reads what.

Whatever the poem, practice together several times until it flows with the vocal effects you have devised. Then perform the poem for another class or special event. If you have copyright permission or have used poems in the public domain, record the poem and keep the tape with a printed copy of the poem or load the recording into a computer audio file and type in the poem's words.

Resources

 Web Site:

Choral Reading Method. 5 Dec. 2002. Community Consolidated School District 21, Wheeling, IL <www.d21.k12.il.us/dept_instr/langarts/parentinfo/choral_rdg.html>.

Giggle Poetry. Meadowbrook Press. 5 Dec. 2002.<www.gigglepoetry.com/> (Click on Poetry Fun.)

Ramsey, Inez. *Forms of Poetry for Children.* James Madison U. 5 Dec. 2002
  <http://falcon.jmu.edu/~ramseyil/poeform.htm>.

Walker, Lois. *Scripts For Schools*. 5 Dec. 2002. <www.scriptsforschools.com>.
  (Choose "Free Teacher Aides" from drop-down menu)

Reader's Theater

A more formal dramatization method is Reader's Theater (RT). RT is reading aloud dramatically to communicate a story. While choral reading is as much for the participant as the listener, RT is designed for an audience. As with choral reading, your arrangements can be as simple or elaborate as time, budget, and imagination allow. Participants hold scripts and read. Simple costuming, such as hats or masks to depict different characters, is often used. Simple set pieces, such as tables or stools, can suggest trees, houses and other locales. RT usually has more solo lines than choral reading.

Commercial scripts are available from a variety of sources. (See Scripts for Schools <www.scriptsforschools.com> and Aaron Shepherd's Web site <www.aaraonshep.com>.) Creating your own script takes some time and effort, but also allows you to customize your production for your students and audience. To write your own script, choose an appropriate story poem. Consider how many strong readers you have and give them the main parts. The rest of the class can participate as "the chorus." Here's an example:

RT scripting for "The Owl and the Pussycat"
by Edward Lear

Characters: Owl — owl mask with feathers
  Pussycat — cat mask, tail
  Pig — pig mask
  Turkey — turkey mask, span of feathers pinned on back
  Chorus — everyone else

Set: Two chairs

Verse 1
Owl and Pussycat take seats. Chorus stands behind them.

Chorus: The Owl and the Pussycat went to sea
  In a beautiful pea-green boat;
  They took some honey, and plenty of money,
  Wrapped up in a five-pound note.
  The Owl looked up to the stars above,
  And sang to a small guitar.

Owl: (looks up, strums "air guitar") O lovely Pussy, O Pussy, my love,
  What a beautiful Pussy you are,

Chorus: (softly) and **Pig:** You are!
What a beautiful Pussy you are!

Verse 2
Chorus: Pussy said to the Owl,

Pussy: (looks adoringly at Owl) You elegant fowl,
How charmingly sweet you sing!
Oh! Let us be married; too long we have tarried:
But what shall we do for a ring?

Chorus: They sailed away, for a year and a day,
To the land where the bong tree grows;
And there in a wood a Piggy-wig stood, (Enter Pig)
With a ring at the end of his nose,
His nose,

All: His nose,
With a ring at the end of his nose.

Verse 3
Owl: "Dear Pig, are you willing to sell for one shilling
Your ring?"

Chorus: Said the Piggy

Pig: I will.

Chorus: So they took it away, and were married next day (enter Turkey)
By the Turkey who lives on the hill.
They dined on mince and slices of quince,
Which they ate with a runcible spoon;
And hand in hand, on the edge of the sand,
They danced by the light of the moon,

Owl: The moon,

Pussy: The moon,

Owl and Pussy: They danced by the light of the moon

After you have practiced, perform your RT for other classes and school and community groups.

Resources

Web Site:

Shepherd, Aaron. *Author Online! Aaron Shepherd's Home Page.* 5 Dec. 2002. <www.aaronshep.com>

Walker, Lois. *Scripts For Schools.* 5 Dec. 2002. <www.scriptsforschools.com>. (Choose "Free Teacher Aides" from drop-down menu).

These sites have links to other RT sites.

Full Dramatization

A full dramatization of a story poem takes RT a step further. Purists would insist that students memorize their lines, but it is also acceptable for them to hold their scripts and read, if necessary. A dramatization can include more costuming and scenery, but those are not essential. The main difference between RT and a full dramatization is in the action itself. A play is acted out.

Here is a dramatized version of "The Owl and the Pussycat":

"The Owl and the Pussycat"
by Edward Lear

Characters: Owl – owl mask with feathers or full owl costume
Pussycat – cat makeup, black bodysuit, tail, and ears
Pig – pink pajamas with feet, pig snout, ears, and curly tail
Turkey – turkey mask, span of feathers pinned on back
Chorus – other animals, dressed according to their species

Set: Boat: side of canoe cut out of corrugated cardboard box taped to two chairs facing each other. Painted green.
Sail: gift wrap tube with white triangular construction paper
Bong tree: Hat tree with cardboard leaves attached
Stars and Moon: Cut from cardboard and hung from the ceiling
Table or picnic basket and blanket

Props: jar of honey, wad of play money, ukulele, ring, dishes and silverware

Act I
Boat and chairs are on stage. Sail is hidden, lying behind boat.
Act opens with Chorus standing behind boat.

Chorus: The Owl and the Pussycat went to sea

(Owl and Pussycat enter with honey, money, and ukulele. Owl helps Pussycat into boat.

> They took some honey, and plenty of money
> Wrapped up in a five-pound note.
> The Owl looked up to the stars above,
> And sang to a small guitar,

Owl: (looks up, strums ukulele) O lovely Pussy, O Pussy, my love,
What a beautiful Pussy you are,
You are

Chorus: (softly) and Pig: You are!
What a beautiful Pussy you are!

Act 2

Chorus: Pussy said to the Owl,

Pussy: (looks adoringly at Owl) You elegant fowl,
How charmingly sweet you sing!
Oh! Let us be married; too long we have tarried:
But what shall we do for a ring?

Chorus: They sailed away, for a year and a day,

(Owl hoists sail. Owl and Pussy enjoy the ride.)
> To the land where the bong tree grows;

(Owl and Pussy stand. Chorus removes boat and chairs; place Bong tree where boat was.)

> And there in a wood a Piggy-wig stood, (Enter Pig)
> With a ring at the end of his nose,
> His nose,

All: His nose,
With a ring at the end of his nose.

Act 3

Owl: "Dear Pig, are you willing to sell for one shilling
Your ring?"

Chorus: Said the Piggy

Pig: I will.

(Pig gives ring to Owl.)

Chorus: So they took it away, and were married next day (enter Turkey, carrying open book.)

By the Turkey who lives on the hill.

(Owl and Pussy stand before Turkey as in wedding. Chorus acts as attendants and guests. Turkey may add line "I now pronounce you husband and wife." Owl and Pussy may kiss. Others clap or cheer. Chorus brings in table or picnic supplies.)

They dined on mince and slices of quince,
Which they ate with a runcible spoon;

(All enjoy "wedding reception" pretending to eat.)

And hand in hand, on the edge of the sand,

(Owl and Pussy take hands and dance)

They danced by the light of the moon,

Owl: The moon,

Pussy: The moon,

(Chorus flanks Owl and Pussy and joins the dance.)

All: They danced by the light of the moon.

All stand in a row abreast and bow

Resources

 Web Site:

Many commercial suppliers of children's plays exist. Here are a few sources:

Baker's Plays Publishing Co.<www.bakersplays.com>.

Contemporary Drama Service <www.contemporarydrama.com>.

Pioneer Drama Service, Inc.<www.pioneerdrama.com>.

Samuel French, Inc.<www.samuelfrench.com>.

Chapter 6   *I Feel Pretty: Feelings*

Previous chapters have shown students how words and phrases can impart information, entertain, and tell a story. Students who gain an understanding of how words express emotions will have positive ways to manage their feelings. "Learning words that identify feelings is essential to a child's personal and social development. A vocabulary of emotions is one of the keys that opens the door to personal well-being and successful involvement in our social world," Pat Schniederjan, school psychologist, said (Schniederjan, Pat. "Children's Words." E-mail to Jane Heitman. 20 Nov. 2002). Students' feelings can be validated by reading poems that reflect their feelings. Students can learn that they are not alone or strange in feeling the way they do.

Discuss feelings, emotions, and moods with students. Write some emotion words on the board. Use the lists below, create your own, and have students create their own for the activities to follow.

Poetry suggestions:

Happiness

"Afternoon on a Hill" by Edna St. Vincent Millay (Ferris 269)

"Barter" by Sara Teasdale (Ferris 21)

"The Dunce" by Jacques Prevert (Berry 64)

"A Little Song of Life" by Lizette Woodworth Reese (Ferris 18)

"The Sun" by John Drinkwater (Ferris 262)

"Wind" by James Stevenson (Stevenson 45)

"Written in March" by William Wordsworth (Hale 225)

Sadness

"Chelsea, January 1985-December 1996" by James Stevenson (Stevenson 62)

"Crying" by Galway Kinnell (Hale 122)

"House. For Sale" by Leonard Clark (Prelutsky *Random* 162)

"Rebecca's Reminder" by Mattie J.T. Stepanek (Stepanek 37)

"Since Hanna Moved Away" by Judith Viorst (Hale 123)

"Song" by John Keats (Ferris 289)

Loneliness

"Daffodils" by William Wordsworth (Ferris 218)

"I'm Alone in the Evening" by Michael Rosen (Prelutsky *Random* 142)

"Lone Dog" by Irene Rutherford McLeod (Ferris 155)

Anger

"Brother and Sister" by Lewis Carroll (Hale 81)

"I Wonder Why Dad is so thoroughly Mad" by Jack Prelutsky (Prelutsky *New* 11)

"I'm in a Rotten Mood" by Jack Prelutsky (Prelutsky *New* 142)

"The Quarrel" by Eleanor Farjeon (Ferris 41)

"Sulk" by Felice Holman (Prelutsky *Random* 121)

"What Someone Said When He Was Spanked on the Day Before his Birthday" by John Ciardi (Prelutsky *Random* 139).

Peacefulness

"Keziah" by Gwendolyn Brooks (Prelutsky *Random* 120)

"The Lake Isle of Innisfree" by William Butler Yeats (Ferris 464)

"Night" by William Blake (Ferris 53)

"Night Creature" by Lilian Moore (*Sing* 121)

"Peace" by Yannis Ritsos (Berry 68)

Hope

"About Wishing" by Mattie J.T. Stepanek (Stepanek 39)

"Crocus" by James Stevenson (Stevenson 50)

"Dreams" by Langston Hughes (Prelutsky *Random* 225)

"Hold Fast Your Dreams" by Louise Driscoll (Ferris 22)

"Hope is the Thing with Feathers" by Emily Dickinson (Hale 357)

"I Heard a Bird Sing" by Oliver Herford (Hale 249)

"Listen to the Mustn'ts" by Shel Silverstein (Silverstein *Where* 27)

"Morning Song" by Sennur Sezer (Berry 69)

"A New Hope" by Mattie J.T. Stepanek (Stepanek 61)

"Tents" by James Stevenson (Stevenson 42)

~Fear

"Afraid of the Dark" by Shel Silverstein (Silverstein *Where* 159)

"Diving Board" by Shel Silverstein (Silverstein *Falling* 24)

"Fear" by Shel Silverstein (Silverstein *A Light* 136)

"I'm Bold, I'm Brave" by Jack Prelutsky (Prelutsky *New* 133)

"Life Doesn't Frighten Me" by Maya Angelou (Hale 108)

"My Sister is a Sissy" by Jack Prelutsky (Prelutsky *New* 138)

"Nightmare" by Siv Widerberg (Berry 80)

"The Scarecrow" by Christian Morgenstern (Berry 77)

"To a Squirrel at Kyle-Na-No" by W.B. Yeats (Ferris 167)

"When I Have Fears that I May Cease to Be" by John Keats (Hale 355)

"Why Run?" by Norah Smaridge (Prelutsky *Random* 106)

~Confidence

"Be Like the Bird" by Victor Hugo (Ferris 280)

"I'm Nobody" by Emily Dickinson (Prelutsky *Random* 128)

"Me" by Walter de la Mare (Ferris 5)

"Song of Greatness" Chippewa Indian song, (Ferris 24)

"The Voice" by Shel Silverstein (Silverstein *Falling* 38)

"The Wonderful World" by William Brighty Rands (Ferris 260)

Like/Love

"Chocolate, Chocolate" by Arnold Adoff (Prelutsky *Random* 149)

"Deaf Donald" by Shel Silverstein (Silverstein *A Light* 143)

"How Many, How Much" by Shel Silverstein (Silverstein *A Light* 8)

"Hug o' War" by Shel Silverstein (Silverstein *Where* 19)

"Just Me, Just Me" by Shel Silverstein (Silverstein *Where* 152)

"Love" by William Jay Smith (Hale 141)

"My Star" by Robert Browning (Ferris 266)

"Oh, Teddy Bear" by Jack Prelutsky (Prelutsky *New* 110)

"Poem" by Langston Hughes (Hale 141)

"Sun and Shade" by Michael Mondo (Berry 39)

"To a New Baby" by Strickland W. Gilliland (Hale 91)

"Two People" by Eve Merriam (Prelutsky *Random* 143)

"Valentine" by Shel Silverstein (Prelutsky *Random* 38)

"Won't You?" by Shel Silverstein (Silverstein *Where* 112)

Dislike/Hate

"For Sale" by Shel Silverstein (Silverstein *Where* 52)

"Hard to Please" by Shel Silverstein (Silverstein *Falling* 74)

"I Hate Harry" by Miriam Chaikin (Prelutsky *Random* 104)

"I Saw a Little Girl I Hate" by Arnold Spilka (Prelutsky *Random* 103)

"I'm Disgusted with my Brother" by Jack Prelutsky (Prelutsky *New* 128)

  In the activities below, students will read a wide range of poems from various time periods. They will apply language knowledge to interpret and evaluate poems. They will appreciate reading and creating poems, and pursue information for personal interests.

~Mood Quilt

Materials needed: 10-inch construction paper squares, art supplies, tape

Supports AASL Standards 1, 2, 3, 4, 5, 6, 9

Supports NCTE Standards 1, 2, 3, 4, 6, 8, 11, 12

Cut 36 10-inch construction paper squares of coordinating colors. Give each student one square. Help students use library and Web resources to find a poem that reflects their moods. They should decorate their square with the poem and appropriate artwork, using art supplies and computer programs and sign their names. Tape the poems together on the back, so that the front resembles a quilt pattern. Display on the wall or bulletin board. Label "The Many Moods of (name of class)."

Extension
Have students use library and Web resources to find information about quilt patterns. Have them try to create their Mood Quilt in a simple quilt pattern.

~Opposing Moods

Materials needed: Art supplies, computer with word processing and graphics programs, colored card stock, string or ornament hangers

Supports NCTE Standards 1, 2, 3, 4, 6, 8, 11, 12

Ask students what are the opposite emotions of happy (sad), angry (peaceful), fear (confidence), love (hate). Add others, as appropriate. Either choose one pair of emotions or have students work in groups, with each group working on one pair of emotions. Help students use library and Web resources to find one poem for each emotion. Help students copy, print, or use computer software to type the poems. Use art supplies and computer graphics to decorate poems. Mount poems back-to-back on a piece of colored card stock and hang so that both sides can be read.

~In the Mood

Supports AASL Standards 1, 2, 3, 4, 5, 6, 8, 9

Supports NCTE Standards 1, 2, 3, 4, 5, 6, 8, 11, 12

Help students use library and Web resources to find poems displaying designated emotions. Students can also write their own emotion-packed poems. Selected poems will create their own Mood Poetry Book. Either make one book or folder for each emotion, or one book containing several emotions, with each emotion a separate chapter or file.

Students can illustrate the poems. If poems are original or are in the public domain, a print copy can be kept in the library and posted to the school Web page or in a computer file on the school network.

Emotion Motion

Supports AASL Standards 1, 2, 3, 5, 6, 9

Supports NCTE Standards 1, 2, 3, 4, 6, 8, 11, 12

Have students work in groups of three or four. Help them use library and Web resources to choose a poem evoking a strong emotion. Collaborate with the physical education teacher to help students design movements appropriate to the emotion to accompany the poem. When groups are ready, have them read and perform their motions for the class.

Emotional Temperature

Materials needed: Paper thermometer display as described below, selected poems

Supports AASL Standards 1, 2, 3, 5, 6, 9

Supports NCTE Standards 1, 2, 3, 4, 6, 8, 11, 12

Draw a thermometer for display on a wall or bulletin board. Mark degrees along the side. Label the bottom "Calm" and the top "Red Hot Anger." Put students in groups of three. Distribute poems reflecting peace and anger, a different poem to each group. (Or help students use library and Web resources to find poems.) Have each group read and talk about the poem. Then have them give the poem a temperature. When they are ready, have each group read their poem to the class and tell what temperature they chose and why. Then they should put the poem on the wall or bulletin board near the thermometer's degree mark they have chosen.

Happiness Scale

Materials needed: Large smiley face, large frowning face, selected poems

Supports AASL Standards 1, 2, 3, 5, 6, 9

Supports NCTE Standards 1, 2, 3, 4, 6, 8, 11, 12

Make a large smiley face on one end of a wall or bulletin board with a number 5 below it. Make a frowning face on the other end with a number 1 below it. Write numbers 2, 3, and 4 evenly in-between. Put students in groups of three. Distribute poems reflecting happiness and sadness, a different poem to each group. (Or help students use library and Web resources to find poems.) Have each group read and talk about the poem. Then have them give the poem a happiness rating, from 1 to 5, with 5 being the happiest. When they are ready, have each group read their poem to the class and tell what rating they chose and why. Then they should put the poem on the wall or bulletin board near their rating.

~Emote Yourself

 Materials needed: Selected poem

Supports AASL Standards 2, 3, 4, 5, 6, 9

Supports NCTE Standards 1, 3, 4, 6, 11, 12

Read to the class a poem that evokes strong emotion. Then have students write original poems evoking the same emotion. Have them begin their poems with the first line of the poem you read. Students may volunteer to share their poems aloud or display them. Some good starting lines are:

Happiness
"Glad that I live am I" from "A Little Song of Life" (Ferris 18)

"I told the sun that I was glad" from "The Sun" (Ferris 262)

"I will be the gladdest thing" from "Afternoon on a Hill" (Ferris 269)

"Life has loveliness to sell" from "Barter" (Ferris 21)

Sadness
"Crying just a little bit" from "Crying" (Hale 122)

"I had a dove and the sweet dove died" from "Song" (Ferris 289). Allow students to change the word "dove" if another word better describes their experience.

Loneliness
"I wandered lonely as a cloud" from "Daffodils" (Ferris 218). Allow students to change the word "cloud" if another word better describes their experience.

"I'm alone in the evening" from "I'm Alone in the Evening" (Prelutsky *Random* 142). Allow students to change the word "evening" if another word better describes their experience.

Anger
"I quarreled with my brother" from "The Quarrel" (Ferris 41). Allow students to change the word "brother" if another word better describes their experience.

"I'm in a rotten mood today" from "I'm in a Rotten Mood" (Prelutsky *New* 142).

Peacefulness
"Peace is the odor of food in the evening" from "Peace" (Berry 68).

Hope
"Hold fast your dreams!" from "Hold Fast Your Dreams" (Ferris 22).

Fear
"I'm bold, I'm brave, I know no fear" from "I'm Bold, I'm Brave" (Prelutsky *New* 133)

"I'm Reginald Clark, I'm afraid of the dark" from "Afraid of the Dark" (Silverstein *Where* 159). Allow students to insert their own names in place of "Reginald Clark."

Confidence
"There's a voice inside of you" from "The Voice" (Silverstein *Falling* 38)

Like/Love
"I love you, I like you" from "Love" (Hale 141)

"Oh, Teddy Bear, dear Teddy" from "Oh, Teddy Bear" (Prelutsky *New* 110). Allow students to change "Teddy Bear" to another endeared object.

"Sweet Marie, she loves just me" from "Just Me, Just Me" (Silverstein *Where* 152). Allow students to change "Marie" to another name that reflects their experience.

Dislike/Hate
"I Saw a Little Girl I Hate" from "I Saw a Little Girl I Hate" (Prelutsky *Random* 103). Allow students to change "Little Girl" to a description that reflects their experience.

"I'm disgusted with my brother" from "I'm Disgusted with my Brother" (Prelutsky *New* 128). Allow students to change "my brother" to a description that reflects their experience (sister, friend, aunt, etc.)

Glossary

Acrostic a poem in which the initial letter of each line spells a word when read vertically

Alliteration repeated initial consonant sounds, usually within a line of poetry

Anagram a word or phrase made by scrambling letters within a word or phrase; a puzzle of scrambled letters

Anapest a poetic metrical foot of one set of two unaccented syllables and one accented

Assonance repeated vowel sounds within a line of poetry

Blank verse a poetry form of unrhymed iambic pentameter

Choral reading group reading of a poem, usually with some special effects

Chorus repetition within a poem or song, usually four lines between verses

Cinquain a five-line poem in which with first line is a two-syllable word giving the title, the second line is four syllables describing the title, the third line is six syllables expressing an action related to the title, the fourth line is eight syllables expressing a feeling related to the title, and the fifth line is two or three syllables giving a different word for the title.

Concrete Poetry poetry written to form a shape, usually of the thing the poem is about

Connotation the suggested meaning of a word, in addition to its literal meaning

Dactyl a poetic metrical foot of one set of an accented syllable and two unaccented syllables

Diamante a seven-line diamond-shaped poem, whose form is one noun in contrast to line seven, two adjectives that describe line one, three gerunds relating to line one, four nouns, the first two relate to line one, the second two relate to line seven, three gerunds that relate to line seven, two adjectives that describe line seven, one noun in contrast to line one

Dramatic monologue a poem written to someone, with no reply from that someone

Etymology the study of word history

Foot the basic metric poetic unit of rhythm

Free verse poetry with no distinct rhythm or rhyme pattern

Haiku a Japanese poetry form of three lines, usually about nature; the first line is seven syllables, the second line is five syllables, the third line is seven syllables

Iamb a poetic metrical foot of one set of one unaccented and one accented syllable

Iambic Pentameter five sets of iambs

Imagery sensory experience expressed through language; it often illustrates an abstract quality by describing concrete thing

Metaphor a comparison using "is," in which the "is" may be direct or implied

Meter regular poetic rhythm

Narrative poetry poetry that tells a story

Onomatopoeia words that sound like what they are, for example, "buzz"

Personification giving non-human things human qualities

Point of view who is narrating the poem

Readers' Theater a script, read aloud to an audience

Refrain a repeated phrase or line

Rhyme a sound-alike word; words with accented syllables, usually endings, that have the same vowel sound.

Rhyme scheme the rhyme pattern of a verse or poem

Rhythm the rise and fall of accented and unaccented syllables throughout a phrase.

Simile a comparison using "like" or "as"

Slang informal, non-standard vocabulary, often used by a particular group

Standard English English uniform in its spelling, meaning, and punctuation, used by educated speakers and writers of the language

Style the way in which a piece is written

Tanka a Japanese poem of 31 syllables, written to mark an occasion; in English, the lines have five syllables, seven, five, seven, seven

Trochee a poetic metrical foot of one set of one accented syllable and one unaccented

Bibliography

~Resources To Use With Students

American Folksongs & Spirituals, Milwaukee, WI: Hal Leonard, 1996.

Baron, Virginia Olsen. *The Seasons of Time, Tanka Poetry of Ancient Japan*, NY: Dial, 1968. (OP)

Berry, James, ed. *Around the World in Eighty Poems*, San Francisco, CA: Chronicle, 2001.

Ciardi, John. *You Read to Me, I'll Read to You*, NY: Harper, 1987.

Clements, Andrew. *Frindle*, NY: Aladdin, 1998.

Cohn, Amy L., ed. *From Sea to Shining Sea*, NY: Scholastic, 1993.

Cole, Joanna, comp. *Six Sick Sheep: 101 Tongue Twisters*, NY: Scholastic, 1993.

Cole, William, comp. *Oh, What Nonsense!*, NY: Puffin, 1990.

Creech, Sharon. *Love that Dog*, NY: HarperCollins, 2001.

Dakos, Kalli. *The Bug in Teacher's Coffee and Other School Poems*, NY: Harper, 1999.

Ferris, Helen, comp. *Favorite Poems Old and New*, NY: Doubleday, 1957.

Fleischman, Paul. *Big Talk: Poems for Four Voices*, Cambridge, MA: Candlewick, 2000.

—. I am Phoenix: *Poems for Two Voices*, NY: Harper, 1989.

—. Joyful Noise: *Poems for Two Voices*, NY: Harper, 1988.

Fletcher, Ralph J. *Poetry Matters: Writing a Poem from the Inside Out*, NY: HarperCollins, 2002.

Garrison, Webb B. *What's in a Word: Fascinating Stories of More than 350 Everyday Words and Phrases*, Nashville, TN: Rutledge, 2000.

Gollub, Matthew. *Cool Melons—Turn to Frogs! The Life and Poems of Issa*, NY: Lee, 1998.

Hale, Glorya. *Read-Aloud Poems for Young People*, NY: Black Dog & Leventhal, 1997.

Hall, Donald, ed. *The Oxford Illustrated Book of American Children's Poems*, NY: Oxford U P, 1999.

Harley, Avis. *Leap Into Poetry,* Honesdale, PA: Wordsong Boyds Mills Press, 2001.

Harrison, Michael and Christopher Stuart-Clark. *The Oxford Treasury of Children's Poems*, NY: Oxford U P, 1999.

Hesse, Karen. *Out of the Dust*, NY: Scholastic, 1999.

Hummon, David. *Animal Acrostics*, Nevada City, CA: Dawn, 1999.

Jackson, Holbrook, ed. *The Complete Nonsense of Edward Lear*, NY: Dover, 1976.

Janeczko, Paul B., *Favorite Poetry Lessons*, NY: Scholastic, 1998.

—. *How to Write Poetry,* NY: Scholastic, 1999.

—, sel. *The Place my Words are Looking for: What Poets Say about and through their Work*, NY: Atheneum, 1990.

—, comp. *Poetry from A to Z: A Guide for Young Writers*, NY: Simon, 1994.

—, sel. *A Poke in the I,* Cambridge, MA: Candlewick, 2001.

—, comp. *Seeing the Blue Between: Advice and Inspiration for Young Poets*, Cambridge, MA: Candlewick, 2002.

—, sel. *Stone Bench in an Empty Park*, NY: Grolier, 2000.

—. *Writing Funny Bone Poems*, NY: Scholastic, 2001.

Katz, Alan. *Take Me Out of the Bathtub and Other Silly Dilly Songs*, NY: McElderry, 2001.

Katz, Bobbi. *A Rumpus of Rhymes*, NY: Dutton, 2001.

Koch, Kenneth and Kate Farrell. *Talking to the Sun: An Illustrated Anthology of Poems for Young People*, NY: Metropolitan Museum of Art and Holt, 1985.

Lewis, Richard. *In a Spring Garden*, NY: Dial, 1989.

Longfellow, Henry Wadsworth and Christopher Bing, ill. *The Midnight Ride of Paul Revere*, Blodgett, OR: Handprint, 2001.

Milne, A.A. *Now We Are Six*, NY: Dutton, 1992.

—. *When We Were Very Young*, NY: Dutton, 1988.

O'Neill, Mary. *Hailstones and Halibut Bones*, reissue ed., NY: Doubleday, 1989.

Opie, Iona and Peter Opie, eds. *The Oxford Book of Children's Verse*, NY: Oxford U P, 1999.

Peter, Paul and Mary. *Peter, Paul, and Mommy,* Warner, audio CD released 1990.

Poetry for Young People Series

    Browning, Robert. *Robert Browning*, NY: Sterling, 2001.

    Carroll, Lewis. *Lewis Carroll*, NY: Sterling, 2000.

    Dickinson, Emily. *Emily Dickinson*, NY: Sterling, 1994.

    Frost, Robert. *Robert Frost*, NY: Sterling, 1994.

    Kipling, Rudyard. *Rudyard Kipling*, NY: Sterling, 2000.

    Lear, Edward. *Edward Lear*, NY: Sterling, 2001.

    Longfellow, Henry Wadsworth. *Henry Wadsworth Longfellow*, NY: Sterling, 1998.

    Millay, Edna St. Vincent. *Edna St. Vincent Millay*, NY: Sterling, 1999.

    Poe, Edgar Allan. *Edgar Allan Poe*, NY: Sterling, 1995.

    Sandburg, Carl. *Carl Sandburg*, NY: Sterling, 1995.

    Shakespeare, William. *William Shakespeare*, NY: Sterling, 2000.

    Stevenson, Robert Louis. *Robert Louis Stevenson*, NY: Sterling, 1998.

    Whitman, Walt. *Walt Whitman*, NY: Sterling, 1997.

    Yeats, William Butler. *William Butler Yeats*, NY: Sterling, 2002.

Porter, Daniel. *Cat Got Your Tongue: The Real Meaning Behind Everyday Sayings*, NY: Troll, 1999.

Prelutsky, Jack. *The New Kid on the Block*, NY: Greenwillow, 1984.

—, comp. *The Random House Book of Poetry*, NY: Random, 1983.

Rosenbloom, Joseph and Mike Artell. *The Little Giant Book of Tongue Twisters*, NY: Sterling, 1999.

Rosenbloom. *World's Toughest Tongue Twisters*, NY: Sterling, 1987.

Scholastic Children's Dictionary, NY: Scholastic, 2002.

Schnur, Steven. *Autumn: an Alphabet Acrostic*, NY: Clarion, 1997.

—. *Spring: an Alphabet Acrostic*, NY: Clarion, 1999.

—. *Summer: an Alphabet Acrostic,* Boston, MA: Houghton, 2001.

—. *Winter: an Alphabet Acrostic*, NY: Clarion, 2002.

Schwartz, Alvin. *Busy Buzzing Bumblebees and Other Tongue Twisters*, NY: Harper, 1982.

Seuss, Dr. *Oh Say Can You Say?* NY: Random, 1979.

Silverstein, Shel. *Falling Up*, NY: Harper, 1996.

—. *A Light in the Attic*, NY: Harper, 1981.

—. *Where the Sidewalk Ends*, NY: Harper, 1974.

Simon, Carly. *Hotcakes*, Electra, audio CD released 1990.

Sing a Song of Popcorn, Every Child's Book of Poems, NY: Scholastic, 1988.

Stepanek, Mattie J.T. *Journey Through Heartsongs*, NY: Hyperion, 2001.

Stevenson, James. *Popcorn*, NY: Greenwillow, 1998

Stevenson, Robert Louis. *A Child's Garden of Verses*, NY: Franklin Watts, 1987. (Many editions of this book exist. This one has illustrations by Brian Wildsmith.)

Terban, Marvin. *It Figures! Fun Figures of Speech*, NY: Clarion, 1993.

—. *Scholastic Dictionary of Idioms*, NY: Scholastic, 1998.

Thayer, Ernest Lawrence and Christopher Bing, il. *Casey at the Bat*, Blodgett, OR: Handprint, 2000.

Umstatter, Jack. *Where Words Come From*, Danbury, CT: Watts, 2002.

Winter, Jeanette. *Emily Dickinson's Letters to the World*, NY: Farrar, 2002.

Worth, Valerie. *All the Small Poems and Fourteen More*, NY: Farrar, 1996.

Young, Sue. *Scholastic Rhyming Dictionary*, NY: Scholastic, 1997.

Resources for the Library Media Specialist and Teacher

Armour, Maureen W. *Poetry, The Magic Language*, Englewood, CO: Teacher Ideas Press, 1994.

Buzzeo, Toni. *Collaborating to Meet Standards: Teacher/Librarian Partnerships for K–6*, Worthington, OH: Linworth, 2002.

Collom, Jack and Sheryl Noethe. *Poetry Everywhere, Teaching Poetry Writing in School and in the Community*, NY: Teachers and Writers Collaborative, 1994.

Glandon, Shan. *Integrating Technology: Effective Tools for Collaboration*, Worthington, OH: Linworth, 2002.

Handler, Marianne and Ann S. Dana. *Hypermedia as a Student Tool*, Englewood, CO: Libraries Unlimited, 1998.

Heard, Georgia. *Awakening the Heart: Exploring Poetry in Elementary and Middle School*, Portsmouth, NH: Heinemann, 1999.

Holmes, Vicki L. and Margaret R. Moulton. *Writing Simple Poems: Pattern Poetry for Language Acquisition*, Cambridge: Cambridge U P, 2001.

Information Power: Building Partnerships for Learning, Chicago: American Library Assn., 1998.

Kazemek, Francis E. and Pat. *Enriching our Lives: Poetry Lessons for Adult Literacy Teachers and Tutors*, Newark, DE: IRA, 1996.

Koch, Kenneth. *Rose, Where Did You Get That Red?* NY: Vintage, 1990.

— and Kate Farrell. *Sleeping on the Wing*, NY: Vintage, 1981.

—. *Wishes, Lies, and Dreams*, NY: Harper, 2000.

Kowit, Steve. *In the Palm of Your Hand: a Poet's Portable Workshop*, Gardiner, ME: Tilbury, 1995.

Lloyd, Peta, et. al., eds. *The Literacy Hour and Language Knowledge: Developing Literacy Through Fiction and Poetry*, London: Fulton, 1999.

McCracken, Robert A. and Marlene J. McCracken. *Stories, Songs, and Poetry to Teach Reading and Writing: Literacy through Language*, Chicago: ALA, 1986. (OP)

Morice, Dave. *The Adventures of Dr. Alphabet: 104 Unusual Ways to Write Poetry in the Classroom and the Community*, NY: Teachers and Writers Collaborative, 1995.

Perrine, Laurence. *Sound and Sense*, 10th ed., NY: International Thompson, 2000.

Pinksy, Robert and Maggie Dietz, eds. *Americans' Favorite Poems*, NY: Norton, 2000.

Sedgwick, Fred. *Writing to Learn: Poetry and Literacy Across the Primary Curriculum*, NY: RoutledgeFalmer, 2001.

Tiedt, Iris McClellan. *Tiger Lilies, Toadstools, and Thunderbolts, Engaging K–8 Students with Poetry*, Newark, DE: IRA, 2002.

Zweizig, Douglas L. and Dianne McAfee Hopkins. *Lessons from Library Power: Enriching Teaching and Learning*, Englewood, CO: Libraries Unlimited, 1999.

∾Web sites

Academy of American Poets. *Poets.org*. 2002. Academy of American Poets. 5 Dec. 2002. <www.poets.org/>. Information about American poets, poems, audio.

American Association of School Librarians Home Page. 21 Nov. 2002. American Library Assn. 5 Dec. 2002 <www.ala.org/aasl/>.

American Library Association. Home Page. 5 Dec. 2002. <www.ala.org>.

Baker, Frank, ed. *Media Literacy Clearinghouse*. 30 June 1999. 5 Dec. 2002. <www.med.sc.edu/medialit>. Has articles, lessons, background information about media literacy.

Baker's Plays Online. 5 Dec. 2002 <www.bakersplays.com>. Scripts.

Choral Reading Method. 5 Dec. 2002. Community Consolidated School District 21, Wheeling, IL <www.d21.k12.il.us/dept_instr/langarts/parentinfo/choral_rdg.html>. Tips on choral reading.

Creative Writing for Teens. 2002. About.com. 5 Dec. 2002 <http://teenwriting.about.com>. Writing tips for young people.

Dakos, Kalli. Home page. 6 Nov. 2002. 5 Dec. 2002 <www.kallidakos.com>. Read Kalli's school poems, students' poems, and write to Kalli.

Diamante Structure. School District of Siren, Siren, WI. 5 Dec. 2002 <www.siren.k12.wi.us/hs/academics/Englishrocks/English%2011/poetry-diamante.html>.

Favorite Poem Project. Boston U, Poetry Soc. of America, and Library of Congress. 5 Dec. 2002 <www.favoritepoem.org>. "For Teachers" section has lesson plans, activities, online videos of poetry reading.

Giggle Poetry. Meadowbrook Press. 5 Dec. 2002 <www.gigglepoetry.com/>. Poetry activities, contests, games, links to poets.

Grimes, Linda Sue. "Langston Hughes' "Harlem: A Dream Deferred" *Classic Poetry for Students Who Hate Poetry!* 5 Dec. 2002 <www.geocities.com/classicpoetry/lhdreamdeferred.html.>

Guilford, Chuck. *Poetryexpress*. 10 July 2002. 5 Dec. 2002 <www.poetryexpress.org>. Has poetry assignments, activities, glossary.

Hurst, Carol and Rebecca Otis. *Carol Hurst's Children's Literature Site*. 1999. 5 Dec. 2002. < www.carolhurst.com>. Has book reviews, library and teaching ideas, monthly newsletter.

Infogrames. Home page. 19 Feb. 2003. 2001 <http://us.infogrames.com/>. Search games to find Scrabble®.

International Reading Association Home Page. 2002. International Reading Assn. 5 Dec. 2002 <www.reading.org>.

Lancashire, Ian, ed. *Representative Poetry Online*. ver. 3 1912–2002. U of Toronto. 5 Dec. 2002 <http://eir.library.utoronto.ca/rpo>.

Laurent, Hillary L. *Discovering Robert Frost.* La Crosse, WI: Viterbo U. 5 Dec. 2002. <www.viterbo.edu/academic/ug/education/edu250/hllaurent.htm>. Web lesson on Frost.

Magnetic Poetry Home Page. 2002. 5 Dec. 2002 <www.magpo.com>. Create poetry online with Magnetic Poetry's online Kids Kit

Meriwether Publishing Ltd. *Contemporary Drama Service Home Page*. 2001. 5 Dec. 2002. <www.contemporarydrama.com>. Scripts.

Melanie and Mike. *Take Our Word for It*. 25 Nov. 2002. 5 Dec. 2002 <www.takeourword.com/theory.html>. Etymology.

National Council of Teachers of English. *Standards for the English Language Arts*. Nov. 2002. 5 Dec. 2002. <www.ncte.org/standards/standards.shtml>.

National Council of Teachers of English Home Page. Nov. 2002. 5 Dec. 2002 <www.ncte.org>.

Online Poetry Classroom. 2002. American Academy of Poets. 5 Dec. 2002 <www.onlinepoetryclassroom.org>. Find poems and poets, curriculum and lesson plans, teacher resource center.

Opp-Beckman, Leslie. *Pizzaz!*... Diamante Poems. 17 Apr. 2002. U of OR. 5 Dec. 2002 <www.uoregon.edu/~leslieob/diamantes.html>.

Oxford English Dictionary. 2002. Oxford U. 5 Dec. 2002. <www.oed.com/public/welcome/>. Full access is subscription only, but parts are open to guests.

PBS. *PBS Kids*. 2002. Public Broadcasting Service. 5 Dec. 2002 <http://pbskids.org>. Has language games, songs, videos for kids, section for parents and teachers.

Peter, Paul, and Mary. 2002. 5 Dec. 2002. <www.peterpaulandmary.com>. Contains lyrics and music.

Pioneer Drama Service. 2002. <www.pioneerdrama.com>. Scripts.

Poetry Collections, Poetic Forms & Styles, and Poets. 1 Dec. 2002. Web English Teacher. 5 Dec. 2002 <www.webenglishteacher.com/poetry.html>. Click on Poetry Forms for lesson plans and activities.

Ramsey, Inez. *Forms of Poetry for Children*. James Madison U. 5 Dec. 2002 <http://falcon.jmu.edu/~ramseyil/poeform.htm>.

Rhyme Zone. 2002. Lycos.com. 5 Dec. 2002 <www.rhymezone.com>. Online rhyming dictionary.

Samuel French, Inc., Home Page. 1998. 5 Dec. 2002 <www.samuelfrench.com>. Scripts.

Scholastic. *Annie's Rhyme Time*. 2002. 5 Dec. 2002 <http://teacher.scholastic.com/annie/>. Scholastic Teacher section, Annie's Riddle Game.

Scholastic Home Page. 2002. 5 Dec. 2002 <www.scholastic.com>. Has sections for kids, families, and teachers with word games, contests, and online activities.

Shepherd, Aaron. *Author Online! Aaron Shepherd's Home Page*. 5 Dec. 2002 <www.aaronshep.com>. Scripts and writing tips for young people.

Staley, C. T., ed. *Tongue Twister Database*. 1 July 2002. 5 Dec. 2002 <www.geocities.com/Athens/8136/tonguetwisters.html>.

Suzuki, Ryo, Ed. *Children's Haiku Garden*. 9 Nov. 2002. 5 Dec. 2002 <www.tec-net.or.jp/~haiku/>. Read haiku from children around the world. Submit your own.

Teachers and Writers Collaborative Home Page. 2002. Teachers and Writers Collaborative. 5 Dec. 2002 <www.twc.org>. Reading, writing, and teaching information.

TeenLit.com Home Page. 19 Oct. 2002. 5 Dec. 2002 <www.teenlit.com>. Workshop section has writing tips.

ThinkQuest, Inc. Home page. 2002. 5 Dec. 2002 <www.thinkquest.org>. Offers technology-based educational activities and programs.

Tucker, Bob. *Grandpa Tucker's Rhymes and Tales*. 2 Nov. 2002. 5 Dec. 2002 <www.night.net/tucker/>. Stories, poems, and songs; instruction on rhyming.

Wacky Web Tales, Kids' Place. 1996-2002. Houghton Mifflin Co. 5 Dec. 2002 <www.eduplace.com/tales/index.html>. Create computer generated tales, reinforce parts of speech.

Walker, Lois. *Scripts For Schools*. 5 Dec. 2002 <www.scriptsforschools.com>. Scripts, free resources and tips.

Wilton, David. *Wilton's Word and Phrase Origins*. 4 Sept. 2002. 5 Dec. 2002 <www.wordorigins.org>. Etymology.

Young People's Poetry Week. 1998–2002. Children's Book Council. 5 Dec. 2002 <www.cbcbooks.org/html/poetry_week.html>. Has activities, links, poetry book recommendations.

Young, Roxyanne, Ed. *SmartWriters.com*. 2002. 5 Dec. 2002 <www.smartwriters.com>. Information on books, reading, and writing with sections for kids and educators.

Author/Title Index

A

"A Canner Exceedingly Canny" 30
A Light in the Attic 95, 96
A Poke in the I 48
A Rumpus of Rhymes 36
"About Wishing" 94
Adoff, Arnold 96
"Adventures of Isabel" 18, 83
"Afraid of the Dark" 95, 100
"Afternoon on a Hill" 20, 93, 99
"Alas, Alack!" 83
Alexander, Cecil Francis 61
American Folksongs & Spirituals 32
Angelou, Maya 95
Animal Acrostics 3
"Animal Fair" 32
"Anyone Lived in a Pretty How Town" 76
"April Rain Song" 61
"Arithmetic" 70
Armour, Maureen W. 61, 85
Artell, Mike 30
"At the Zoo" 64
Autumn: an Alphabet Acrostic 3

B

"Bagpipe who Didn't Say No" 64
Bainton, George 21
"Barbara Frietchie" 79
Baron, Virginia Olsen 14
"Barter" 93, 99
"Be Like the Bird" 95
Belloc, Hillaire 20, 83
"Bells" 35
Benet, Rosemary and Stephen Vincent 79
Bennet, Rowena 32
Berry, James 61, 64, 93, 94, 95, 96, 100
"Betty Botter" 30
Big Talk 86
Bishop, Morris 30
Blake, William 32, 33, 61, 94
Branch, Anna Hempstead 47, 48
"Brook" 32

Brooks, Gwendolyn 94
"Brother and Sister" 94
Browning, Elizabeth Barrett 33
Browning, Robert 96
"Buckingham Palace" 64
Bug in Teacher's Coffee and Other School Poems 61, 63, 103
Burns, Robert 58
Busy Buzzing Bumblebees and Other Tongue Twisters 30
"Butterfly's Day" 61
Buzzeo, Toni xii

C

Carroll, Lewis 6, 7, 19, 83, 94
Casey at the Bat 82, 83
"Cataract of Ladore" 32, 34
Chaikin, Miriam 96
"Chanson Innocente" 64
"Charge of the Light Brigade" 79, 83
Chase's Calendar of Events 14, 79
"Chelsea, January 1985–December 1996" 93
Chippewa Indian Song 95
"Chocolate, Chocolate" 96
Ciardi, John 76, 94
Clark, Leonard 93
Clement, Andrew 6
"Cloud" 61
Coatsworth, Elizabeth 25
Coffin, Robert P. Tristram 32
Cohn, Amy 69, 77, 79
Cole, Joanna 30
Cole, William 7
Collom, Jack xi, 85
"Colors live" 62
"Contrary Mary" 7
Cool Melons—Turn to Frogs! The Life and Poems of Issa 10
"Cotton-Eye Joe" 32
"Creature in the Classroom" 83
"Cremation of Sam McGee" 83
"Crocodile" 19
"Crocodile's Toothache" 83

Author/Title Index 113

"Crocus" 94
"Crying" 93, 99
cummings, e e 32, 44, 64, 76

D

"Daddy Fell into the Pond" 25, 83
"Daffodils" 58, 94, 99
Dakos, Kalli 61, 63
Dayre, Sydney 84
de la Mare, Walter 47, 61, 83, 95
"Deaf Donald" 96
Dickinson, Emily xi, 47, 58, 61, 94, 95
"Diving Board" 95
"Dreams" 61, 94
"Dredge" 58
Drinkwater, John 93
Driscoll, Louise 94
"Duel" 82
"Dunce" 93

E

"Eagle" 18, 32
"Erie Canal" 79
"Eletelephony" 7
Eliot, T.S. 44

F

Falling Up 95, 96, 100
Farjeon, Eleanor 94
Farrell, Kate 10
Favorite Poems Old and New 7
"Fear" 95
Ferris, Helen 7, 30, 32, 33, 35, 44, 48, 53, 56, 61, 64, 67, 70, 79, 82, 83, 84, 93, 94, 95, 96, 99, 100
Field, Eugene 82
Fleischman, Paul 86
"Fog" 51, 53
"For Sale" 96
"Foul Shot" 83
Frindle 6
Frost, Robert 64, 69, 70, 84

G

Garrison, Webb B. 23, 29
"Gift" 44
Gilliland, Strickland W. 96

Glandon, Shan xii
"Going to the Zoo" 77
Gollub, Matthew 10

H

Hailstones and Halibut Bones 50, 51, 62
Hale, Glorya 7, 18, 20, 21, 25, 28, 32, 33, 36, 42, 44, 47, 48, 53, 58, 61, 64, 76, 79, 80, 83, 84, 93, 94, 95, 96, 99, 100, 103
Happiness 64
"Hard to Please" 96
"Harlem: A Dream Deferred" 61
Harrison, Michael 30
"Have You Ever Seen?" 28
Herford, Oliver 95
"Highwayman" 83
Hodgson, Ralph 83
Hoey, Edwin A. 83
"Hold Fast Your Dreams" 94, 100
Holman, Felice 94
"Homework" 25
"Hope is the thing with Feathers" 94
"Hotcakes" 80
"House. For Sale" 93
"How Do I Love Thee?" 33
"How Many, How Much" 96
Howitt, Mary 83
"Hug o' War" 96
Hughes, Langston 42, 44, 61, 94, 96
Hugo, Victor 95
Hummon, David 3

I

I am Phoenix 86
"I Hate Harry" 96
"I Hear America Singing" 70
"I Heard a Bird Sing" 95
"I Saw a Little Girl I Hate" 96
"I Wonder Why Dad is so Thoroughly Mad" 94
"I'm Alone in the Evening" 94, 99
"I'm Bold, I'm Brave" 95, 100
"I'm Disgusted with my Brother" 96, 100
"I'm in a Rotten Mood" 94, 100
"I'm Nobody" 95
"I've Got an Incredible Headache" 58
"If" 84

"in Just-" **44, 64**
Information Power **xii**
Issa **9**
It Figures! Fun Figures of Speech **23, 29**

J

"Jabberwocky" **6, 7**
"Jack and Jill" **73**
"Jack Sprat" **73**
Jackson, Holbrook **18**
Janeczko, Paul B **10, 48**
"January" **19**
"Jest 'Fore Christmas" **82**
Joyful Noise **86**
"Jumping Rope" **70**
"Just Me, Just Me" **96, 100**
Justice, Donald **47**

K

Katz, Bobbi **35, 36**
Keats, John **93, 95**
"Keziah" **94**
King, Ben **42, 44**
Kinnell, Galway **93**
Kipling, Rudyard **84**
"Kitten at Play" **44**
Koch, Kenneth **10**
Kunnas, Kirsi **61**

L

"Lake Isle of Innisfree" **94**
"Laughing Song" **61**
"Lazy Jane" **64**
Lear, Edward **7, 83, 86, 87–88, 89–91**
"Lesson for Mama" **84**
Lewis, Richard **9**
"Li'l Liza Jane" **32**
"Life Doesn't Frighten Me" **95**
A Light in the Attic **95, 96**
Lindsay, Vachel **53, 64, 67**
Lipton, Lenny **77**
"Listen to the Mustn'ts" **95**
"Listeners" **83**
"Little Bo-Peep" **73**

Little Giant Book of Tongue Twisters **30**
"Little Orphant Annie" **42, 83**
"Little Song of Life" **93, 99**
"Lone Dog" **33, 94**
Longfellow, Henry Wadsworth **79, 82, 83**
"Love" **84, 96, 100**
Lowell, Amy **47, 61**

M

"Macavity: the Mystery Cat" **44**
"Maggie and Milly and Molly and May" **32**
"Matilda who Told Lies, and was Burned to Death" **20, 83**
Maugham, W. Somerset **47**
McCord, David **35**
McCracken Robert A. **63**
McLeod, Irene Rutherford **33, 94**
"Me" **95**
Merriam, Eve **34, 96**
"Microscopic Topic" **61**
"Midnight Ride of Paul Revere" **79, 82**
Millay, Edna St. Vincent **20, 93**
Milligan, Spike **7**
Milne, A.A. **64, 83**
Mistral, Gabriela **64**
Mondo, Michael **96**
"Monkeys and the Crocodile" **82**
"Moon's the North Wind's Cooky" **53**
Moore, Lilian **94**
Morgenstern, Christian **95**
"Morning Song" **95**
"Mother to Son" **42**
"Mungle and the Munn" **83**
"My Love is Like a Red Red Rose" **58**
"My Mother's Hands" **47, 48**
"My Shadow" **20**
"My Sister is a Sissy" **95**
"My Star" **96**
"Mystery" **48**

N

"Nancy Hanks" **79**
Nash, Ogden **18, 58, 83**
New Kid on the Block **61, 83, 94, 95, 96, 100**
"New Hope" **95**
Nichols, Grace **64**
"Night" **94**

"Night Creature" **94**
"Night Stuff" **47**
"Nightmare" **95**
Noyes, Alfred **25, 83**

O

"O Captain! My Captain!" **79**
O'Neill, Mary **50, 51, 62**
Oh Say Can You Say? **30**
"Oh, Teddy Bear" **96, 100**
Oh, What Nonsense! **7**
"On the Ning Nang Nong" **7**
"On the Porch" **47**
Opie, Iona **32, 34, 42, 44**
"Opposites" **36**
"Owl and the Pussycat" **83, 86, 87–88, 89–91**
Oxford English Dictionary **25, 29**
Oxford Treasury of Children's Poems **30**

P

"Pan and the Potatoes" **61**
"Pancake" **80**
"Pancake Collector" **80, 84**
"Panther" **58**
Parrish, Connie **xi**
"Pasture" **64, 84**
"Paul Revere's Ride" **83**
Paxton, Tom **77**
"Peace" **94, 100**
"Peanut-Butter Sandwich" **64**
Perrine, Laurence **35, 69**
Peter Paul and Mommy **77**
"Peter Piper" **29**
Peter, Paul, and Mary **77**
Pinsky, Robert **44**
"Pirate Story" **44**
"Pobble Who Has No Toes" **7**
Poe, Edgar Allan **35**
"Poem on the Neck of a Running Giraffe" **48**
"Poem" ("As the cat" ...) **44**
"Poem" ("I loved my friend") ... **44, 96**
"Pop Corn Song" **56**
"Potatoes' Dance" **64, 67**
Prelutsky, Jack **7, 19, 33, 34, 42, 48, 58, 61, 69, 70, 80, 83, 84, 93, 94, 95, 96, 100**
Prevert, Jacques **93**

"Puff, the Magic Dragon" **77**
"Puppy and I" **64, 83**

Q

"Quarrel" **94, 100**

R

Random House Book of Poetry for Children **7, 19, 70, 83, 93, 94, 95, 96, 100**
Rands, William Brighty **95**
Read-Aloud Poems for Young People **7**
"Rebecca's Reminder" **93**
Reese, Lizette Woodworth **93**
Richards, Laura E **7, 82**
Riley, James Whitcomb **42, 46, 83**
Ritsos, Yannis **94**
"Rocking" **64**
Roethke, Theodore **61**
Rosen, Michael **94**
Rosenbloom, Joseph **30**
Ross, A.B. **48**
"Row, Row, Row Your Boat" **32**
Rumpus of Rhymes **36**

S

Sandburg, Carl **47, 53, 70**
"Sarah Cynthia Sylvia Stout Would not Take the Garbage Out" **25**
"Scarecrow" **95**
Schniederjan, Pat **93**
Schnur, Steven **3**
Scholastic Children's Dictionary **23, 26, 29**
Scholastic Dictionary of Idioms **23, 29**
Scholastic Rhyming Dictionary **17**
Schwartz, Alvin **30**
"Sea Shell" **47, 61**
"Sea Timeless Song" **64**
"Seal" **48**
Service, Robert **83**
Seuss, Dr. **16, 30, 69, 70**
Sezer, Sennur **95**
Shakespeare, William **35, 46, 69**
Shelley, Percy Bysshe **61**
Silverstein, Shel **25, 42, 48, 64, 69, 70, 80, 83, 95, 96, 100**

Simon, Carly **80**
"Since Hanna Moved Away" **93**
Sing a Song of Popcorn, Every Child's Book of Poems **94**
Six Sick Sheep: 101 Tongue Twisters **30**
"Skunk" **32**
"Sloth" **61**
Smaridge, Norah **95**
Smith, William Jay **48, 84, 96**
"Snake" **47**
"Snowflake" **47, 61**
"Song" **93, 99**
"Song of Greatness" **95**
"Song of the Jellicles" **44**
"Song of the Pop-Bottlers" **30**
"Song of the Train" **35**
"Song: Hark, Hark!" **35**
Southey, Robert **32, 34**
"Spider and the Fly" **83**
Spilka, Arnold **96**
Spring: an Alphabet Acrostic **3**
Stepanek, Mattie J.T. **93, 94, 95**
Stevenson, James **48, 58, 61, 93, 94, 95**
Stevenson, Robert Louis **20, 33, 44**
Stone Bench in an Empty Park **10**
"Stopping by Woods on a Snowy Evening" **70**
"Storm" **58**
Stuart-Clark, Christopher **30**
"Sulk" **94**
Summer: an Alphabet Acrostic **3**
"Sun" **93, 99**
"Sun and Shade" **96**
"Sweet Betsy from Pike" **77**
"Swift Things are Beautiful" **25**

Tagore, Rabindranath **44**
"Tale of Custard the Dragon" **83**
Talking to the Sun: An Illustrated Anthology of Poems for Young People **10**
Teasdale, Sarah **93**
Tennyson, Alfred, Lord **18, 32, 79, 83**
"Tents" **95**
Terban, Marvin **23, 29**
"That Cat" **42, 44**
Thayer, Ernest Lawrence **82, 83**

"There Is No Frigate" **58**
"This Land is Your Land" **69**
"Three Blind Mice" **32**
"Tiger" **32, 33**
"Time, You Old Gypsy Man" **83**
"To a New Baby" **96**
"To a Squirrel at Kyle-Na-No" **95**
"Travel" **33**
Turner, Nancy Byrd **7, 21, 56**
Twain, Mark **21**
"Two in Bed" **48**
"Two People" **96**
"Tyger" **33**

Updike, John **19**
"Upstairs" **64**

"Valentine" **42, 96**
Viorst, Judith **93**
"Voice" **95, 100**

"Walrus and the Carpenter" **83**
Wells, Carolyn **30**
"What in the World?" **34**
"What Someone Said When He Was Spanked on the Day Before his Birthday" **94**
What's in a Word: Fascinating Stories of more than 350 Everyday Words and Phrases **23, 29**
"When I Have Fears that I May Cease to Be" **95**
When We Were Very Young **64**
Where the Sidewalk Ends **48, 64, 70, 80, 83, 95, 96, 100**
Whitman, Walt **70, 79**
Whittier, John Greenleaf **79**
"Why Run?" **95**
Widerberg, Siv **95**
Wilbur, Richard **36**
Williams, William Carlos **44**

"Wind" **61, 93**
Winter: an Alphabet Acrostic **3**
"Witch of Willowby Wood" **32**
"Won't You?" **96**
"Wonderful World" **95**
"Words" **21**
Wordsworth, William **44, 58, 93, 94**
World's Toughest Tongue Twisters **30**
"Written in March" **93**

"Yankee Doodle" **69**
Yarrow, Peter **77**
Yeats, William Butler **94, 95**
Yolen, Jane **25**
You Read to Me, I'll Read to You **76**
Young, Sue **17**

Subject Index

American Association of School
   Librarians (AASL) Information
   Literacy Standards **xii, 1, 2, 3, 6, 9, 10, 11,
      13, 14, 16, 17, 18, 19, 20, 21, 23, 24, 25, 28,
      31, 32, 34, 35, 36, 37, 39, 41, 42, 44, 45, 46,
      47, 48, 49, 50, 51, 53, 54, 55, 58, 60, 62, 63,
      64, 66, 67, 69, 71, 73, 75, 76, 77, 79, 80, 82,
      84, 85, 97, 98, 99**
acrostics **2–3**
adapting activities **xi**
alliteration **29–33, 45**
almanacs **14**
alphabet **1–7, 16–17, 49**
anagrams **3–5**
anapest **68, 98**
anger **94, 100**
antonym **36–39**
assonance **33–35**
atlases **25–26**
blank verse **69**
characters **80–81, 87–91**
choral reading **85–86**
chorus **68, 77, 87–91**
cinquain **12–14**
collaboration **xii, 9**
   class **xi, 1, 4–5, 10, 14–15**
   group **1, 2, 11, 13, 15, 18–19, 37–39**
   with art teacher **2, 6, 10, 44, 50, 60, 67, 82, 84**
   with computer technician **2, 15, 39, 44, 67, 75, 82, 84**
   with kindergarten teacher **75, 76**
   with language arts teacher **12, 47–48, 58–60, 66, 75**
   with life skills teacher **56–58, 79–80**
   with math teacher **41, 49**
   with music teacher **32, 46, 69, 71, 78**
   with physical education teacher **70, 98**
   with science teacher **50, 51, 53–55, 56–58, 63, 66**
   with social studies teacher **14–15, 25–27, 60, 69, 79–80**
computer use **5, 6, 13, 17–18, 19, 34–35, 39, 41, 44, 45, 46, 53–54, 60, 66, 67, 71, 75, 77, 78, 82, 84, 86, 97–98**

concrete poetry **47, 48–50**
confidence **95, 100**
connotation **21–25**
context **6–7, 20**
dactyl **68**
diamante **36–42**
dictionary (ies) **6, 11, 16, 21–28, 37, 39**
dislike/hate **96, 100**
display suggestions **xii, 2, 10–11**
dramatic monologue **83–85**
dramatization **85, 91**
emotion(s) **93–100**
encyclopedias **51**
English, formal **45–46**
   standard **23–24**
   usage **16, 42–46**
etymology **25–29**
fear **95, 100**
feet **68–69**
friendship **44**
haiku **9–11**
happiness **64, 93, 98–99**
historical poems **79**
hope **94, 100**
iamb **68–69**
image(s) **9, 10, 47**
Infogrames **5**
jump rope rhymes **70**
Kidspiration® **45**
language patterns **18–19, 20, 68–69, 76–77**
like/love **84, 96, 100**
limericks **18**
loneliness **94, 99–100**
Magnetic Poetry® Kids' Kit **77**
meaning **9, 24–25**
metaphor **50–58**
meter **68–69**
mood **33, 35, 42, 44–45, 85–86, 97–98**
narrative poem **77–91**
National Council of Teachers of English
   (NCTE) standards **xii, 1, 2, 3, 6, 9, 10, 11, 13,
      14, 16, 17, 18, 19, 20, 21, 23, 24, 25, 28, 31,
      32, 34, 35, 36, 37, 39, 41, 42, 44, 45, 46, 47,
      48, 49, 50, 51, 53, 54, 55, 58, 60, 62, 63, 64,**

66, 67, 69, 71, 73, 75, 76, 77, 79, 80, 82, 84, 85, 97, 98, 99
news story 75
newspaper 51–53, 75
nonsense poems 6–7
nursery rhyme(s) 15, 73–76
onomatopoeia 35–36
pancakes 79–80
peace 94, 98, 100
personification 61–63
phonics 6–7
phrase 47, 71
plot 80–82
poetic devices 45
point of view 83–85
prefix(es) 9, 11–12
principal 15, 41, 49, 66, 71
pronunciation 6–7, 9, 16, 34
rap music 71
Reader's Theater 87–89
reading comprehension 73
refrain 15, 63–68, 77
repetition 63–68, 77
rhyme(s), (-ing) 15–20, 29–30, 45
rhyme scheme(s) 18–19
rhyming dictionaries 15, 19

rhythm 29, 45, 68–71
sadness 93, 97, 99
scene 80–82
Scrabble® 5
Scripts for Schools 85, 87
setting 80, 82
Shepherd, Aaron 87
simile 58–61
slang 16, 21–24
slang dictionaries 21–24
spelling 2–5, 11, 16, 19, 25–28, 34, 77
story (ies) 73–91
story poem(s) 73–91
style 42–46, 60–61
suffix(es) 9, 11–12
syllable(s) 9–20, 34, 68, 70
synonym 24, 32–33
tanka 14–15
theme 80–82
thesaurus(i) 21–23, 39
tongue twister(s) 29–32
trochee 68–69
vocabulary 2, 3, 4, 11, 19, 26, 28, 32, 35, 77
Wacky Web Tales 13
Word order 76–77
words 35–46

About the Author

Jane Heitman, a former school library media specialist and teacher, currently manages the interlibrary loan unit at Mesa State College. She has worked in the education field for 25 years. She has published poetry, curriculum, activities, and other material for children and teachers in church settings. Originally from South Dakota, she and her husband now live in Grand Junction, CO, where she volunteers in the children's center at the public library.

www.ingramcontent.com/pod-product-compliance
Lightning Source LLC
Chambersburg PA
CBHW080541300426
44111CB00017B/2827